Mamphela Ramphele

Steering by the stars

Being young in South Africa

TAFELBERG

Tafelberg Publishers
28 Wale Street, Cape Town 8001
© 2002 author

Cover design by Doret Ferreira
Cover picture by Cathy Pinnock
Book design by Nazli Jacobs
Set in 9.5 on 13 pt Cheltenham

Printed and bound by Creda Communications, Cape Town
First edition, first printing 2002

ISBN 0 624 04096 8

'... all around us, the intellectual lightships had broken from their moorings, and it was then a new and trying experience. The present generation which has grown up in a new open spiritual ocean, which it has got used to and has learned to swim for itself, will never know what it was to find the lights all drifting, the compasses all awry, and nothing left to steer by but the stars.'

J A FROUDE, in J S Mill,
Essays in Politics and Culture

Acknowledgements

My sincere gratitude to the Carnegie Corporation of New York for the generous funding of the study on which this book is based. It is such generosity that has given encouragement to those on the receiving end of an iniquitous system not to give up. To the Independent Development Trust for its generosity and faithfulness to its mission to help the poorest of poor people. To the Rockefeller Brothers Fund for their faith in an experimental model they supported with a generous grant for running costs of the Youth Centre. To the Anglo-American Chairman's Fund, Genesis Foundation, and Caltex Oil Company for generous donations.

Many thanks to the Wilderness Leadership School for the logistical support for the trails that formed such a vital part of the research process. I am particularly grateful to Andrew Muir for the leadership he provided for the trails and his dedication to make the wilderness areas of South Africa accessible to disadvantaged and marginalised young South Africans. I acknowledge the professional assistance of Margot, Andrew's partner and wife, for capturing the experiences of this study in photographs.

Thanks to all my research assistants and colleagues. Special thanks to Marian Heap, whose meticulousness laid a firm foundation for the surveys. Thanks to Pat Henderson who helped with field trips and interviews. Elizabeth Seabi for her love which sustained the troubled young people through their roughest patches. Prof. Wieland Gevers for standing in for me at difficult community participation meetings to clarify the UCT/Community partnership in building the Youth Centre. His good humour diffused tense moments. To all my colleagues at the University of Cape Town who helped with the logistics of planning and building the Youth Centre, especially Julian Elliott. To Tessa Lewin and Lashias Ncube for helping with the literature search, especially Lashias, who bore the brunt of checking and rechecking sources. Finally, to my two sons who generously shared their mother with other young people even when it was inconvenient to do so.

Contents

ABBREVIATIONS

ANC – African National Congress
TRC – Truth and Reconciliation Commission
CASE – The Community Agency for Social Enquiry
COSATU – The Congress of South African Trade Unions
IDT – Independent Development Trust
NGO – Non-governmental organisation
PPA – Planned Parenthood Association
SHAWCO – Students' Health and Welfare Centres Organisation
UCT – University of Cape Town
UDF – United Democratic Front
UNICEF – United Nations Children's Fund
UWC – University of the Western Cape

Introduction

This book was inspired by curiosity about the experiences of childhood and youth in poor urban communities, as my own childhood had been spent in rural villages. I also wanted to understand how post-apartheid South Africa was being experienced at the grassroots level by those growing up in poverty. But above all, the greatest inspiration was my love for young people and my belief in their potential to succeed if given the opportunity to identify their talents and play to their strengths.

The stories in this book capture some of the struggles waged by young people of New Crossroads who are not yet benefiting from the fruits of post-apartheid South Africa. Theirs is a life experience bearing all the scars of the legacy of the past. Inadequate social amenities. Overcrowded homes. The daily grind of poverty that undermines the dignity of ordinary citizens and makes for stressful family relationships. Underperforming schools that provide little hope for a better future for them compared to their uneducated parents. Violent homes, schools and streets that add to the general insecurity in New Crossroads as is the case in many other black townships. And yet these are also stories of hope – that eternal burning flame in the souls of so many who refuse to give up.

At the heart of the hope that burns eternal in South Africa's black townships is resilience. Resilience of people who have seen, heard and experienced pain and anguish, but kept hoping for a better tomorrow. It is this resilience that kept family ties tightly knotted together even as the fabric was fraying at the edges under the onslaught of the migrant labour system that separated men from their families. Family life was criminalised and made punishable by imprisonment and deportation back to the 'homelands'. Resilience enabled families to survive on meagre wages and old age pensions, and still send their children to school to give them a better future. It also allowed women to walk tall wearing smiles even as their dignity was trampled upon by abusive male partners who vented their frustration at being treated like 'boys' on their own women and children. Resilient black women also carry the burden of giving priority to looking after other people's children that they may put a plate of food in front of their own who are left to fend for themselves for much of the time. Resilience has made it possible for many black South Africans to retain the generosity of spirit and the wisdom to be prepared to follow the path of reconciliation rather than retribution against those who deliberately impoverished them.

The stories of these young people also tell of the cost of resilience. The self-image battered daily by self-doubt. The suppressed anger against one's parents who for good reasons are often not as forthcoming with truth as they could be. This economy with the truth often strikes at the heart of one's identity. Many of these young people are frequently unsure of the identities of their biological parents. Some have had nasty surprises sprung on them about siblings they knew nothing about. There is also anger at being physically and emotionally abused at home, at school and in the streets. Fear of failure accompanies one's daily life. Bewilderment abounds about the causes of continuing deprivation in post-apartheid South Africa. Questions are being whispered about the ability of black people to take charge and make a success of democratic governance given failures in so many parts of the African continent. There are urgent questions about the future and their own position within a more inclusive society in which they remain excluded from the benefits of full citizenship.

Unemployment remains the biggest thief of hope amongst young people. The recent Mesebetsi Labour Force Survey shows that those with tertiary education have a 98 per cent chance of being employed whereas those with only secondary school-level education are overly represented amongst the 45 per cent unemployed. This group of New Crossroads young people, with only one exception, belongs to that category of secondary school leavers who remain without suitable jobs. They have little prospect of new job opportunities. The few new jobs the economy is able to create either require high-level skills or are in the unskilled category. The majority of the fifteen remain unemployed. Only one has a good stable clerical job. A few are grateful to be employed as unskilled labourers.

The book is also a plea. It is a plea to South Africa to listen to the voices of young people. They are not just the future but the present.

The South African population is very young. Young people in the fifteen- to thirty-five-year age group constitute almost 35 per cent of the population of 42 million people. Young black people make up 78 per cent of that segment. The majority of young black South Africans share the same hopes, anxieties, fears, bewilderment, and questions about their future as the storytellers in this book. What is remarkable is that these young people have not yet given up on adults. Adults have failed them at many levels in recent history. During the apartheid era parents could not protect their own children against police harassment and the ravages of poverty. In the post-apartheid society poor parents still seem marginal to decision making affecting bread-and-butter issues in society.

In almost every case it is a woman who has kept these young people's hope alive. Women as single parents. Women as effective heads of households with husbands who are not able or willing to assume their responsibilities as partners. Women as grandmothers left to carry the burden of child rearing without the necessary social support except the social pension of R620 per month. Women as members of the extended family who pitch in when children are left with no available parent. It is even women as total strangers who establish supportive bonds to keep children safe and reasonably cared for. In some cases it is young women as siblings who provide each other with mutual support.

The troubling social question raised by these stories of women-centred households and social networks is how this affects young men growing up without positive male role models? This question is made all the more urgent by its disjunction from the male-dominated ethos that permeates all South African cultures, black and white. How do poor young black men model their emergent manhood in the absence of adult male guidance? Or even worse, how do young men shape their own manhood in the presence of negative models: unemployed, alcoholic, abusive and destructive men in such large proportions in their own homes and neighbourhoods? How do young men avoid asking the question: what is wrong with black men? Or how do they respond to the same question if asked? How do young men develop the self-confidence to relate to women if women dominate the provision of so much of their everyday survival needs? How do these young men learn to give as men when men seem to be over-whelmingly recipients of care and not its givers?

Similar complementary questions could be asked of the shaping of young women's psyches in a world in which women assume respon-sibilities for the survival and stability of households and communi-ties without the necessary authority to do so in a male-dominated culture. Fortunately for many young black women there are plenty of positive role models. Women who might be dirt poor and yet carry themselves with a dignity that defies logic. Women who can laugh through pain and anguish. Women who are able to lead even if they are not accorded the authority and recognition of leadership. But at what cost does one laugh through pain?

The misalignment between responsibility and authority bedevils gender relations in many segments of South Africa's social life. Women in their twenties to forties are increasingly opting out of marriage. Many more remain trapped in abusive relationships be-cause their men cannot cope with strong assertive women. But it is this strength that has kept poor black families going for generations. How can young women not be expected to be assertive under such circumstances? But the anger of young men is equally understand-able. They feel trapped in a social dynamic that has failed to provide them with the tools to negotiate relationships with women that go beyond women meeting their physiological and emotional needs. Many have yet to be exposed to loving and mutually caring relation-ships between men and women. How are they expected to manage their fears, insecurities and inadequacies without safe spaces? Is it surprising that many are resorting to the violence they have wit-nessed so often in their lives?

The HIV/Aids epidemic could not have come at a more inopportune time for South Africa. The wounds inflicted by the insults of racial discrimination, and the other socioeconomic sequelae of the apartheid era are still too raw. Many black South Africans have diffi-culty coming to terms with a heterosexually transmitted disease of such immense proportions that affects black people disproportion-ately. It is a cruel irony that it is the migrant labour system, intro-duced and promoted by the mining industry, that served as the en-try point of the epidemic into South Africa from further north. This is yet another nail in the coffin of the family life of black migrant workers in Southern Africa. To add insult to injury, a significant proportion of the returning heroes of the struggle against apartheid also served as an additional entry point. Having been scattered in their youth throughout the world, but largely in Southern Africa, these young and not so young activists also brought back the dreaded disease. More than ten per cent of the population is now infected. The fifteen- to thirty-five-year olds, the most economically active group, bear the largest burden of the disease with about 25 per cent of them infected. Young women are disproportionately affected.

The failure of the post-apartheid government to respond adequately to this catastrophe should be understood against the fear of acknowledging an epidemic that could easily be used to fan the worst racial stereotyping. The mistrust of science that has traditionally been controlled by white people also contributed to ambiguity in the government's policy response. Denying black South Africans access to scientific knowledge was a central feature of apartheid education. The chickens are now coming home to roost. With gender relationships as unequal as they are, and with increasing sexual violence against women and children, HIV/Aids might yet succeed where apartheid failed: snuffing out the flame of hope.

The post-apartheid government must transcend the legacy it inherited and deliver appropriate preventive, promotive and drug treatment to the countless citizens afflicted with HIV/Aids. We must not allow the past to imprison the present and the future.

I had the privilege to see just how little it costs to keep the flame of hope alive and make a difference in the lives of young people. Only one weekend a month over three years spent with sixteen of them gave each one of these young people at least eight opportunities to spend a weekend in the pristine wilderness of the Cape Peninsula. These were weekends during which they could behave like children and be treated with love and care as all children should. They ask for so little. They are so appreciative of any attention given them. The return on investment in them is high, but could be higher over a longer term and with greater depth than I could give during the project.

We also had time to talk about their fears and hopes. Many of them had not had the exposure to nature to know even rudimentary facts about plants and animals. I still remember overhearing a heated argument amongst them about whether or not snakes had legs. In the end they decided to come and ask me to settle the question. A brief explanation of the different classes of animals and where snakes fitted in brightened their eyes and opened their world. Andrew Muir, of the Wilderness Leadership School, spent hours explaining the flora and fauna of the Western Cape. It was gratifying to see the growing interest in nature over time.

South Africa has a marvellous and relatively under-utilised resource. The natural environment constitutes a significant portion of the surface area of the country. The wilderness areas are being increasingly used by both the public and private sectors and are forming a basis for creative partnerships between South Africans across race, class, age and gender. The Great Limpopo Transfrontier Park extends this across national boundaries to build a bridge between South Africa, Mozambique and Zimbabwe. The wilderness provides a levelling space for social intercourse across historical and current divides. It is this resource base that provided the space and context for my enduring relationship with the young people whose stories I capture in this book.

The book strives to retain as much of the voice of the young people as possible. Chapter One sets the scene by depicting the sharp contrasts between the bleak New Crossroads township environment and the exquisite beauty of the Cape Peninsula. Chapters Two and Three provide pen sketches of the main characters in the book. A young woman who succeeded against all odds to become a confident professional and a young man who defied near fatal twin car accidents and much more to finally get a tertiary education. Chapters Four, Five and Six pick up the themes of the experiences of home, the school and the community as important social spaces. Chapter Eight reflects on the challenges of community development in the face of the scarcity of appropriate human capital to manage key institutions. The book concludes with an update of where these young people find themselves now. Theirs are compelling stories.

MAMPHELA RAMPHELE
August 2002

CHAPTER ONE

Like a bulb splitting

I

Once a year – in glorious technicolour – the wild flowers of the Western Cape burst into blossom. It's extraordinary that such vibrancy could grow from the arid semi-desert of the West Coast, but it is precisely because of the harshness of the environment that the colours are so bright. Whenever I see this remarkable occurrence, I am reminded of the poet Maya Angelou's comment about hope: 'In the worst of times, incredibly, that's when hope appears, like a seed, like a bulb splitting. One never knows what it cost a bulb to split, a lily bulb or onion, to split open. And the tendril to come out.'

This image is compelling. It became increasingly so because an important aspect of the project on which this book is based entailed hiking through the wilds of the Western Cape with groups of young people who had grown up in New Crossroads, one of Cape Town's apartheid townships. A harsher urban environment is hard to imagine, yet, over the years, some of these young people have indeed flourished. What I wanted to do was track some successes – and failures – because the lives of young people not only tell us where society has come from but also give us a glimpse into the future. Similarly the ways in which family, school and community have shaped their lives reflect the past, and the consequences of this shaping have profound implications for the future.

So, in 1991, with a team of research assistants, I began a project to find out at what cost the bulb splits.

II

The contrast between picturesque Table Mountain, the leafy southern suburbs and the spectacular Atlantic seaboard with its luxury homes on the one hand, and the bleakness of the sandy Cape Flats on the other, is staggering. The comfort of long avenues of oak trees that line some of the richer suburbs is unknown to those who battle with the frequent sandstorms in the townships. Similarly the smell of the fresh sea breezes that characterise seaboard Cape Town, give way to the choking sewerage smells that hover over the Cape Flats where the city – with its 'out of sight, out of mind' mentality – has chosen to situate its treatment plants. This contrast bears witness to the success of racist planning and development that goes back to the beginning of white settlement at the Cape. It is on these Flats, some fifteen kilometres from the centre of Cape Town, that New Crossroads is to be found. It is here that the young people whose stories I listened to lived.

New Crossroads is part of a larger township, Nyanga, which covers about 330 hectares and provides sites for almost sixty thousand people in just under fifteen thousand households. Within Nyanga there are five distinct areas, each reflecting various historical moments and approaches to urban development. More importantly, each of these areas has different kinds of housing arrangements (formal housing, hostels, site and service areas, informal squatter settlements) with varied access to services (street lighting, roads, water, electricity, sewage, shops etc.) that creates a hierarchy of privileges within the township.

Nyanga was established in the late 1940s in response to overcrowding in Langa, at that time the only African township of Cape Town. This original development consisted of free-standing and semi-detached houses with outside toilets. Subsequently many of these houses were extended, and almost all have backyard shacks with families living in them.

The next major development in Nyanga took place a decade later when government efforts in the Western Cape, particularly in the vicinity of Cape Town, firmly entrenched the area as 'non-African'. One of the central strategies to achieve this was to declare a Coloured Labour Preference Policy for the Western Cape. This notorious policy, announced by the National Party government in January 1955, made it difficult for Africans to be employed in the Western Cape and made it illegal for Africans without employment to live in the region.

In order to effectively implement this policy, the Nyanga Emergency Camp (later renamed KTC) was established in 1956. The purpose was to relocate all African squatters in the Cape Peninsula to KTC while deciding whether individuals could stay, or should be 'removed' to distant 'homelands'. About two thousand sites were established with limited services: one pit latrine for every two families, and a single water tap for every thirty families. KTC remained a low-service squatter camp, housing up to thirty thousand people, until the early 1990s when some upgrading programmes were implemented.

The next major initiative in the area was the opening of single-sex hostels for migrant labour during the 1960s by both government and private employers. A severe shortage of accommodation, as well as a resistance to the impact of the migrant labour system on family life, soon saw hostels providing homes for entire families – in space that was allocated for single individuals.

New Crossroads was developed in the early 1980s, primarily in response to the growing number of illegal squatters. These people were overwhelmingly women from the Eastern Cape who were determined to unite their families which had been torn asunder by the migrant labour system. Although denied the right to work or live in Cape Town, they arrived in large numbers, settled in informal shacks as close to the city centre as possible and simply refused to move. Even in the face of large-scale harassment, intimidation and outright force on the part of the police, the women stayed put. They finally won the battle when, in 1979, the government agreed to build a new township to house the people living in the Crossroads squatter camp. This township was called 'New Crossroads'.

New Crossroads comprises almost two thousand residential sites with brick houses ranging from one to three bedrooms. Many of the houses have gross structural defects. Some have electricity installed by the owners, but others rely on coal or paraffin for lighting and heating. All houses have a stand tap. The majority have inside taps and rudimentary bathroom facilities. The main streets are tarred and lit from high mast-lamps. Most if not all households have backyard extensions to accommodate members of families who cannot fit into the small houses. In addition many families let backrooms to generate extra income to make ends meet.

Despite the inadequacies of the housing on offer in New Crossroads, it is still a desirable location when compared with the other alternatives in Nyanga. Within this particular township the most sought-after form of housing is that of old houses built in the 1940s and 1950s. The vast majority of township residents do not have access to these structures, they have to make do with squatting in the backyard shacks attached to the brick homes.

Understanding New Crossroads in relation to its surrounding areas is important to an understanding of the life stories I was told by the young people. For instance, many of their stories show that frequently entry into New Crossroads was via squatting in KTC as families desperately sought to establish themselves in Cape Town.

Facilities within Nyanga as a whole are sparse with eight primary schools, two secondary schools, three sports grounds, and three community halls. There are some very rudimentary shops selling a variety of goods from fruit, vegetables and meat to cloth and housewares, and some services such as haircutting, shoe repairs, photography, and restaurants. The main taxi rank providing transport to Cape Town city centre is within easy walking distance of most Nyanga residents.

As yet there is no evidence that this shortage of community facilities is being addressed by the new government.

Ironically, despite the severe overcrowding and lack of resources that undermine the quality of education on offer in New Crossroads, young people who have access to schools are part of a privileged sector in this community. This is particularly so for those able to continue their education after primary school although very few young people in Nyanga complete school.

The two secondary schools, Oscar Mpetha High School and Stembele Matiso, are likely to continue to be overcrowded (currently twice as many pupils as they should have) well into the future. Key problems at the first school go beyond the educational issues associated with inadequate facilities. External factors such as noise and violence are acute due to the location of the school close to the local taxi rank. Indeed, there are few, if any, evening or weekend events held at the school because the area is considered 'unsafe' by local residents.

This is hardly the ideal environment within which to educate young people. Consequently many drop out, distracted by the apparent futility of attempting to study under these conditions. Some are prevented from continuing by the harsh economic reality which forces families to make tough choices about who can continue with school and who cannot.

In most other respects, the situation in New Crossroads is much the same as in other townships throughout the country. Most children in New Crossroads will grow up in a household that has between five and nine members. Just under a third of households will be headed by a female. The average 'dependency ratio' – is one to three. Most will live at the level of absolute poverty as defined by the World Bank's measure of under one US dollar per day.

According to a survey conducted at the start of my project, the New Crossroads population numbered slightly more than ten thousand. Most of these people were below the age of thirty-five. A minority were employed, most of them earning less than R350 a month. Education levels were low with under one per cent having any post-secondary qualifications.

III

When I began the research project I could find no records on New Crossroads in the Cape Town Planning Department. It simply did not exist for apartheid's urban planners. It had been relegated to the unknown, poorly kept records of the Ikapa Town Council, an apartheid creation notorious for its inefficiency. To live in a place that is not meant to exist, is to live in a twilight world.

Compounding this reluctance on the part of the state to recognise the existence of New Crossroads, was a complementary desire of many of the New Crossroads residents not to draw attention to themselves. Many were living illegally in Cape Town. Hounded by the police and the policy of 'forced removal', caught in the middle of battles between exploitative war- and shack-lords, survival sometimes depended on the extent to which they were able to avoid being visible. Living in the backyards of friends and relatives, they were the 'unclaimed people'. They went unrecorded during national census enumeration. They were not catered for in the provision of most social services such as health and education.

Forced removal by the apartheid state is an integral part of most African families' histories. Beyond the devastating social and psychological impact such events had on individuals and families, it made the keeping of family histories and documents almost impossible, consequently many were lost, along with other precious possessions, during these forced moves. In addition fire, both accidental and designed, destroyed thousands of homes and possessions in the informal settlements. Rain and floods during the wet Cape winters soaked people and possessions in their shacks and makeshift houses. Birth certificates, marriage contracts, school records, and other important records rarely survived the ravages of the elements. The high level of overcrowding also made the safe keeping of records and documents difficult, often impossible.

While the state is responsible for much of the formal recording of events (such as births and deaths) there are other less formal and more personal ways of keeping records in diaries and journals. But these measures are not available to people who cannot read or write.

IV

It is axiomatic that social science has suffered from the years of racism and the isolation of apartheid South Africa. The will to tackle the big social questions facing the new democracy has been undermined by a number of factors. Apartheid drove many social scientists away from the country, as did the general 'brain drain' that affects the whole continent. Academic boycotts and calls to isolate South Africa as part of the anti-apartheid struggle limited opportunities for social scientists to draw on international scholarship which diminished the quality of the discipline.

The neglect of intellectual development among black South Africans, especially Africans, has created an imbalance between the availability of black researchers and the enormous problems affecting black communities. Knowledge of language, idiom, customs and traditions and their distortions, is an essential tool in tackling social questions which leaves white social scientists, generally unfamiliar with black South African languages, at a disadvantage.

Also, accusations of racism against white people are frequently used to silence criticism from them however well founded and well-meaning. This silencing device has made white academics wary of tackling sensitive social issues. The consequent silence from those who constitute the majority of active researchers robs society of knowledge essential for formulating, implementing and monitoring public policy. We need to confront these issues and create a more open, questioning environment that will strengthen social enquiry.

In addition to these issues, social scientists face inadequate material, as I have pointed out, and more subtle obstacles. In our research we had to deal with the sort of behaviour which has become part of the survival techniques of New Crossroads residents – in fact of most township residents – but which stands in the way of accurate data collection. For instance, the willingness of households to participate in the survey – a response rate of 88 per cent, with only five per cent outright refusals – contrasts starkly with the accuracy of detailed responses to questions. The high level of inaccuracy, particularly relating to income levels and sources of income, reflected the residents' customary practice of basing their answers on a perception of how the information might be used.

One of the strategies of people who have learnt to mistrust authority is either to withhold information altogether or to give misleading information.

As we got to know our sample of forty-eight, and later sixteen households, more information was made available than during the initial survey of 1991. Some of the inaccuracies were substantive, others were minor but affected the data nevertheless.

For example, many households did not disclose their income derived from the rental of backyard shacks, but included the lodgers in their statement of members of the household. The dependency ratios calculated in 1991 may have been overestimated in some cases, while the impressions of the structure and dynamics of some households had to be revised as we got to both observe and be told more accurate details.

As one of the residents put it: 'We give you the information we think you want, but also that which we feel we can afford to give.'

This approach to providing information raises questions about the level of accuracy of survey data in communities where follow-ups to verify the authenticity of responses are not possible. It is going to be important to keep track of changes in attitudes as post-apartheid democracy matures. For instance, how long will it take, I wonder, for mistrust of public institutions to give way to a trusting relationship?

Another example: to help collect information we used a local as a guide and facilitator. Unfortunately, the New Crossroads community was very protective of this person so we were not told about her previous history of unreliability and dishonesty. On the contrary, she came with glowing references. Fairly soon we came to understand that community solidarity was an essential survival strategy.

The most serious consequence of our 'guide's' dishonesty affected our random sample of forty-eight households because it included children of friends or relatives some of whom did not even live in New Crossroads. When children whose names were not on the list arrived for the weekend wilderness trails that I ran as part of the project, she gave plausible reasons as to why the selected children had not turned up. Either there were delays at the schools in letting them out in time for the Friday departure at four o'clock or she hadn't found adults who could give the necessary permission.

We found she was using the weekend trails as a source of patronage to enhance her status in the community by deliberately excluding children from households she did not regard as deserving of her favour. When finally confronted, she adopted a matter-of-fact approach, admitting that she was trying her luck, and it was a pity that we had found her out. Even more disturbing was the attitude of important members of the community whom we had consulted before making the decision to employ her. They were equally casual about it: 'Oh, she has been like that all along, that is why she lost her previous jobs, but we were giving her another chance because she is a gifted person. It's a pity that she does not learn.'

This resonates with my previous work among migrant-labour hostel dwellers. The problems were of a different nature, but with the same root causes. Research was regarded as a resource to be harnessed for patronage and power play as part of the survival strategies of poor people. These problems call into question the appropriateness of community involvement in all levels of research. The idealism behind participatory research as part of the process of empowering people has to be tempered with realism.

V

Given the inadequacy of official statistics for New Crossroads, my initial survey aimed at establishing the demography of the households, and then the health of ten- to fourteen-year-old children attending the three primary schools.

From this information we randomly selected forty-eight households with children between these ages and then established the dynamics within the homes regarding the number of occupants, the physical space and surroundings.

Similar details were noted about the primary schools and, through numerous community meetings called by the New Crossroads Civic Association to discuss youth-related problems in the community, we gathered insight into community politics, interpersonal relations, attitudes to child rearing, as well as people's hopes and fears about the future.

A major challenge was finding ways to encourage a group of adolescents to express themselves freely to adult researchers. At first I gave them diaries and asked them to keep a daily record of their activities and what they had eaten.

Then I organised discussion forums, each taking an entire day at the regional offices of the Wilderness Leadership School, near the scenic Kirstenbosch Gardens. I thought that physically taking a group out of the township would encourage them to express themselves without the fear of retaliation from parents or teachers.

My strategy was to allow them to settle down and become as spontaneous as possible in their discussions with us, although we had questions to guide the flow of conversation through such issues as sexuality, gangs, general violence, and the sort of social networks they had established.

Finally I took groups on weekend trails into the wilderness areas of the Western Cape with the assistance of the Wilderness Leadership School. These trails, regular monthly events between 1991 and the first half of 1993, consisted of eight adolescents, two researchers, a photographer, and a trail leader from the Wilderness Leadership School. Most of the forty-eight adolescents went on at least three trails.

Without doubt the trails provided an ideal opportunity for me to get physically and emotionally closer to these young people. We drove together in a minibus on a Friday afternoon to a camping site and spent the weekend sharing food, conversation, play, walks, and environmental briefings from the trail leader. At the end of the trail each adolescent handed in a weekend journal. Given the fun and sheer difference of the weekend, the Sunday afternoon drive back to Cape Town was inevitably a sad occasion.

The project also included a number of workshops within New Crossroads that involved many more children than the chosen forty-eight to discuss issues relating to their lives.

In 1993, after the project had been running for two years, I selected sixteen households and children from the original forty-eight, as part of a study set to run into their adulthood. The basis on which the sixteen households were selected was not random as I wished to have included in the group a particular mix of ages, gender, family and social backgrounds, and coping abilities – what today's business jargon would call 'risk management strategies'. To achieve this last condition, half of the group was chosen on the basis of extraordinary potential or demonstrated leadership qualities. The balance comprised children at high risk from families racked by domestic violence, alcoholism or any other sign of instability. Most of the children in this group had schooling problems.

Of course my relationship with the sixteen youths taking part in the long-term project was even more intense. Almost all the adolescents in this group went on eight trails each and while the basic format of the trails remained the same, their level of trust in the research team rose. This allowed for more openness and increased our sensitivity towards the individuals.

VI

I chose to use the beautiful natural environment in the Cape Peninsula as a context for this project. I wanted to establish a congenial place and the spectacular mountains and beaches of the Cape Peninsula as well as the numerous natural and planted forests provided a perfect setting. That many of the young people had not had the opportunity until then to enjoy this common wealth was an added incentive. I delighted in seeing their faces light up as we drove deeper into these wilderness areas so close to Cape Town and yet so far for those without the opportunities to reach them. We only had to drive for an hour to find ourselves surrounded by quiet, peace and beauty with no sign of the city's noise and tensions.

The trails were part of my attempt to introduce these young people to the common assets to which they had been denied access.

The Cape Peninsula is part of one of the richest and most biologically diverse floral kingdoms in the world. The three major groupings are the proteas (the country's national flower), ericas and restios. Whether you are looking at the giant protea cone with its deep pink, white and brown contrasting colours or its smaller sisters with their more intense red colours wrapped tightly around the fresh mixture of a white and pale green core, you cannot but be filled with awe.

In the last thirty years the ability of wilderness areas to facilitate team-building exercises has become a commonplace. Walking requires little skill other than basic fitness and can be done by young and old, weak and strong, rich and poor. So I felt it was an ideal place to get to know these young people. The walks also opened up new experiences for them: they could walk alone or in groups. They had the opportunity to choose. A rare circumstance in their normal lives.

Wilderness, too, is a spiritual space. Many troubled souls find solace in it. I had personally experienced its healing powers when, in 1990, I became severely depressed by the turn of political events following Nelson Mandela's release. I retreated to the wilderness to re-establish a connection with my inner self. I had not bargained for the political point scoring that threatened the negotiation process that ended white rule. The jockeying for positions within the various political movements was also a shock to my idealistic attitudes. It was the long walks along the beaches of Simon's Town, the smell of the sea, the unceasing energy of the crushing waves and the security provided by the majestic Hottentots Hollands mountains in the east that restored me. I was forced to confront my insignificance as merely a part of a larger universe. I was able to gain a better perspective on the relationship between my role as an individual and the larger forces at work in the country's history. It was my hope that exposing these young people to the healing power of the wilderness would have a positive effect on them. It was also an opportunity for me to continue my own journey of restoring my inner self.

I used two main bases for our weekend trails. The first was a beach cottage in the Cape Point nature reserve. The second was an open camp site under a cluster of trees in the Steenbras dam nature reserve.

The Cape Point site is about forty minutes from the centre of Cape Town. It is a relaxing drive to the point where the Indian and Atlantic oceans are said to meet. Quite literally I could feel the weight of the city fall away as we went south until the frolicking, elegant young springbok and the more robust bontebok with their distinct white buttocks welcomed us as we drove slowly towards our weekend retreat. The city and the township were left behind.

The beach cottage had three bedrooms with enough bunk beds to accommodate eight youngsters and four minders, a kitchen with a gas stove, bathrooms with flushing toilets, a sitting room, and a large verandah from which we could enjoy the beauty of the sunset and the rise of the moon.

The Steenbras dam area provided a contrasting experience. We drove east for an hour taking the steep Sir Lowry's pass over the Hottentots Holland mountains into thick pine forests interspersed with fields of ericas and fynbos. Here we needed tents as well as sleeping bags to keep warm during the cold nights. The wilderness was much closer here than at Cape Point. We had to fetch our own water from the dam, make a campfire, and find private places to relieve ourselves. The rule was to ensure that we left the site as pristine as we found it.

Here the day was filled with birdsong and the nights were loud with the sounds of insects. The smell was of vegetation: some fresh, some decaying.

The success of these trails owed everything to the professionalism of the Wilderness Leadership School, a non-governmental organisation devoted to using the wilderness to promote better leadership qualities in people. For our purposes the school provided a minibus and a trail guide to help the leader, Andrew Muir. We also had the services of a photographer to document the trips. Funds were raised to equip the young people with walking shoes, waterproof jackets and warm jerseys. Each one also needed a warm sleeping bag and a foam mat.

Sponsorships made provisioning possible as feeding young growing bodies is always a challenge, but feeding inadequately nourished ones requires added skill. Yet within an hour of our arrival Andrew Muir would have conjured up soup, pre-cooked chicken pieces or fish, fresh rolls and a liberal supply of soft drinks and beverages. Breakfast was cereal and milk, fruit and beverages. Saturday lunch was sandwiches, fruit and soft drinks to reward the tired bodies after a long morning walk. A generous supply of sweets was always at hand to boost the blood-sugar levels between meals. The most popular meal was the Saturday braai after a day of walking and playing. The smell of the meat and sausages cooking excited not only the young people, but all the tired bodies around the camp. Repeatedly I decided that nothing tasted better than a braai in the wild.

Andrew and I always indulged in a glass of wine or two while listening to the happy noise of the young people against the backdrop of night sounds. We would review the day's events and the group's reactions to the many new encounters, such as the delight at seeing a new species of plant, or an animal. My joy in watching the young people's growing interest in the world that was unfolding around them was immense. So much happiness for so little effort.

After Sunday breakfast we would take a long walk before a picnic lunch of leftovers. As the day progressed, the mood change in the young people reflected a mixture of satisfaction and sadness at the impending departure. 'Why must we go now? Why can't we stay longer? Is it not possible to arrange for a whole week away?' These were the questions that reflected their heartaches. Many kept their sadness to themselves. Others were just happy that they had been there and could go home to share the experience with family and friends.

These trails enriched me enormously. I got to know my environment, and realised once more that to learn by teaching others is a very special experience. Andrew was an enthusiastic teacher. His knowledge of the flora and fauna was deep and thorough. We got everyone to record their observations of plant or animal life, and later found that most of the entries talked of discovering the environment and its riches. Comments were also made about the enjoyment of food and friendship, and, tellingly, of the freedom from the noise, tensions and violence of township life. In fact many parents commented on the calming effect the trails had on their troubled children.

VII

Telling personal life histories did not come easily to some New Crossroads adolescents. I found wide variations in the ability of individuals to recount the stories that reflected their sense of place in the family, community and the future.

My attempts to introduce diaries and journals as a method of keeping track of chronological data in the individual life histories did not work because of its alien nature. I underestimated the constraints of illiteracy on poor people. Of the total forty-eight diaries I gave out in 1991, less than five were returned at the beginning of 1992 after considerable delays. In many other cases, the adolescents had simply put them away without any entries. In one case, the mother had appropriated the diary to record telephone numbers. There were clearly no Anne Franks among our adolescents. Even sharing the remarkable story of Anne Frank with them did not have the desired effect. I underestimated the impact of a non-literary culture on these young people. Anne Frank could draw on a long literary tradition the young people of New Crossroads were on their own.

However, a touching 'success story' was that of a child with a learning disability who could not write. He made colourful pictures to record daily occurrences at school and important events during the survey. For example, he recorded a long trip with his family to the headquarters of the Zion Christian Church in Morija, Polokwane, in Limpopo Province. In lovely colourful drawings he depicted the minibus in which they travelled and the dancing crowds at the meeting. He also pasted decorations from magazines and postcards in his diary. I was distressed to learn that after the praise we showered on him, one of the children became so jealous that she defaced his diary.

But probably the most disturbing incident concerned a very troubled adolescent whom no one could get to talk about his life. He just sat mute. He had such a difficult relationship with his mother that his anger and bitterness overflowed to all adults. He refused to engage in any open discussion because he saw no point in talking. He did not believe he would be listened to. For him silence was an effective screen against painful relationships with adults. This was how he shut them out of his life.

Silence is a powerful form of protest. This teenager exercised what remained of his power by using it. He was the only one of our group who met a violent death when he was shot dead by his own friends. His silence became final.

The stories I was told gave a voice to those silenced over the years. Of course, giving a 'voice' to marginalised groups is fraught with problems. To what extent can these individual stories tell the story of the group? How do you show the web of connections that lends meaning to the stories of individuals? Which voices do you record? What aspects of the story do you tell?

These are challenges that all social researchers face. I chose to move from the broad picture of the lives of forty-eight boys and girls to a more detailed look at the hopes and anxieties of sixteen individuals, finally focussing on two who achieved the greatest success in the transition to adulthood.

The decision to focus on the two most successful individuals was deliberate. Policy makers and those in positions of authority need to hear the stories of these young people. Documenting the ways in which young people survive – even flourish – within unbelievably harsh and deprived circumstances in which such key factors as the family, school and community repeatedly fail them, may provide useful insights into alternative policy approaches to youth development.

The danger of this approach is that a focus on survivors may provide a false picture of success. I continue to find it a source of great hope for the future that despite all the damage done to the social fabric there are many young people who are succeeding as adults. However, this should not be used as an excuse for official inaction. Success under these adverse circumstances was won at a price.

I hope that the stories will provide some clues in response to Angelou's rhetorical question about what cost is borne by the splitting of the seed to give rise to new life. To me, the cost of survival, let alone success, is far too high for many young people. The burning question is: If success costs young people this much, then how high are the costs to individuals who fail, as well as to the communities which have to share in these costs?

VIII

The sixteen* involved in the long-term project:

Bulelwa was brought up by her mother, matriculated in 1996 and went on to complete a diploma in marketing and banking in 1998.

Bulelani was brought up by his mother, matriculated in 1996 and went on to study engineering at a technikon.

Lolo was cared for by her sister and was studying for her Grade 11.

Dumo, who was raised by his grandmother, passed his Grade 11, but left school before completing matric, and became unemployed.

Lunga was raised by his mother and left school with a Grade 11. In 1998 he started working as an unskilled labourer.

Xola was raised by his mother and was studying for Grade 10 when the project ended.

Mthetheleli, raised by his mother and father, was studying for Grade 11.

Nana was raised by her mother, and was in Grade 12.

Tuleka was raised by her mother, matriculated in 1994 and was in her third year at a technikon in the Transkei.

Thabo was brought up by his mother, achieved a Grade 6 pass and became an unskilled labourer.

Pule was raised by her grandmother and was studying for Grade 11.

Bobo, brought up by her mother, was studying for Grade 11.

Nono was brought up by her mother and was studying for Grade 9.

Tomela left school with a Grade 7 pass when his father left the household and his mother could not afford his schooling. He was unemployed.

Tumi was raised by her mother and was studying for Grade 10.

Phalo was raised by his mother. He was killed in gang violence before the project ended.

* names were changed to protect anonymity

CHAPTER TWO

Bulelwa

A woman with a mission

I

Bulelwa's is a story of resilience and success. I remember her visiting me at home years after I first met her, an attractive, self-assured twenty-year-old woman with a bounce in her step as she approached to embrace me. She had an infectious laugh on her slightly moon-shaped face with keen black eyes which danced each time a smile welled up within her. A full smile or a laugh exposed her uneven teeth and a suggestion that a visit to the dentist was long overdue.

Bulelwa had a strong sense of her own worth. She oozed self-confidence, humour, and a sheer enjoyment of life. She was lovely and at ease in any style of clothing: long African traditional outfits or modern tailor-made outfits from boutiques in suburbia.

These were features that made her stand out in 1991 when I first met her and she was fourteen years old. She was engaging. She was not daunted by the prospect of walking up Table Mountain for the first time with strangers as guides. Nor did the idea of sleeping in a hut on the mountain open to the elements dampen her enthusiasm. She was articulate in both Xhosa (her mother tongue) and English.

Her adolescent body was filling out in 1991 but she was quite comfortable with it. She was curious about the new people she met and did not shy away from asking detailed questions about my background and motivation for getting involved with young people in New Crossroads. She was encouraged to hear that I had come from humble circumstances and yet had never doubted that I could achieve whatever realistic goals I set for myself. We bonded from that point onward.

'You are my role model, I know I will make it,' she said.

II

Bulelwa was born in KTC in 1977. Her family moved to New Crossroads when she was five years old. Like most of the residents of New

Crossroads, her childhood was continually disrupted. This disruption was caused not only by the everyday difficulties of living under apartheid, and the associated violence and upheavals characteristic of many townships in the 1980s, but equally by the difficulties of living in poverty with its related instability and uncertainty.

Bulelwa's self-confidence and determination to succeed against all odds was a family characteristic. Her mother, Mrs Leseka, was born in Cape Town towards the end of the 1940s. She grew up in the shacks at Athlone (before it had been upgraded into a coloured township) because her parents were unable to get a house in the townships set aside for Africans. Life was made more difficult by the Coloured Labour Preference Policy and jobs could only be come by if there were no coloured labourers available. Like many others, her family had to endure intolerable levels of overcrowding and scant social services. To exacerbate matters Mrs Leseka's father was also responsible for supporting his brothers and sisters in the Transkei. Given his low wages, his daughter's education was sacrificed in favour of the survival of the extended family.

MRS LESEKA: I was a member of the Methodist church in Langa. We used to sing in choirs. One day I saw people coming to my home. My father told me that these people wanted me to marry their son. My father had no objections if I wanted to marry. Because I was already grown up, I agreed. So in 1973 I married this man. He was from the Transkei. We lived in KTC.

While we were staying in KTC I went to the township superintendent's office in Nyanga looking for a house because, in 1981, New Crossroads was already built. I had problems at the office because Basonti [the township housing superintendent] kept telling me that there were no houses. He said, 'I do not even want to put you on a waiting list because there are no houses. There are none.'

I woke up one day and said I would not go and see Basonti this time. I wanted to see the senior superintendent. I was referred to a certain Mr Du Toit. I explained everything to him. At that time my husband was in hospital because he had an accident while he was at work. I didn't want my husband to come back to a shack from the hospital because the doctors told me that he wouldn't be able to walk again. He was paralysed from the waist downwards. I explained everything to Du Toit: that my husband was still in hospital, there were no toilets, there was no water. Mr Du Toit said I should come the following morning.

The following morning Mr Du Toit instructed Basonti to give me the keys. Mr Du Toit gave me the house number in New Crossroads where I should go. Basonti didn't give me the keys. He just said he would meet me at the house. I waited there from ten o'clock in the morning until two o'clock without a sign of Basonti. Basonti came after two o'clock. Instead of opening the house and inspecting it before giving me the keys, Basonti got out of the car and threw the keys at the door, without saying a word. He then went back to the car. I just took the keys and said, 'Thank God.' If I hadn't gone to Du Toit I would not have got the keys that day. I was so excited when I got that house.

For Bulelwa the move to New Crossroads offered a period of relative stability. By 1981 there were four children in the Leseka family – Bulelwa, her two elder twin sisters, Rose and Fika, and her younger sister, Pumla. Bulelwa's mother would collect her husband's wages for him while he was in hospital and used this income to support the family.

When Bulelwa's father was discharged from the hospital he came to live with the family in their new house in New Crossroads. Shortly afterwards his company sent him a letter informing him that, as he would be unable to work any more, they would send his pension money. Bulelwa's father consulted a lawyer in Athlone about his case and managed to secure a sum of R11 000 from the pension fund and an additional monthly disability grant of R200. The lawyer also agreed to fight for a lump-sum payment from the third party insurance involved in the accident.

Bulelwa remembered the time after her father's accident as an idyllic period in her childhood when there was always enough food and money for the children. With the lump sum from the pension fund Bulelwa's parents opened a spaza shop at the house where they sold cool drinks and groceries. Mrs Leseka also bought a second-hand truck to transport the grocery stock. Bulelwa was five years old. Their home exuded warmth and pleasant smells of food and fresh flowers.

Yet Bulelwa said little about her father. He did not appear to have been a formative influence in her life.

The idyllic life came to an abrupt end two years later when her father decided to leave them. The wound inflicted by that decision was still raw in Bulelwa when I first met her.

I can only speculate about the reason for Mr Leseka's desertion of his wife and children. Bulelwa did not think that her father had any reason to leave the family. He might well have been experiencing pressure from his parents and other family to share his newly found 'wealth' with them. Mr Leseka might have felt resentful that his wife was 'profiting' from his misfortune. It does seem odd that Mrs Leseka had no idea of the extent of her husband's dissatisfaction with their marriage.

MRS LESEKA: After two full years of nursing my husband, do you hear me? We went to collect money as usual from the lawyer, our monthly money. I was with my husband. The lawyer said that he wanted to see me alone. He told me that when I was talking to the secretary my husband demanded his cheque. He wanted to hear from me why my husband had done this because we usually got the cheque together. I said I didn't know. I didn't think there was anything behind this. When we left the lawyer's office we had a good conversation to clear up misunderstandings between us. He then asked me to drop him at his parents' house in Guguletu. He usually did that and I would drop him and pick him up later. Later I went to fetch him as usual. I didn't notice anything unusual.

The following month when I said that we should go and fetch the money, he said that I could go alone. When I got there the lawyer said, 'No, your husband has the money already!' At the time he wasn't at home. He was at his parents' house in Guguletu. I went straight to the house. I greeted them. Nobody responded. I asked how they were feeling. Nobody responded. I spoke to my husband and said that I had come from the lawyer. 'The lawyer said that you have the cheque already. Would you please give it to me because I need it for the children.' My husband said, 'My father has the cheque.' I said, 'How can your father have the cheque when you have five children? Man, give me the cheque because the children are waiting for me alone at home.'

My husband didn't reply. Then I said, 'Let's go home and talk this through.' My husband's sister came out and opened the gate for me and pulled her brother inside and said that I should go alone.

After hearing the gossip from the neighbours, I learnt that my husband's parents said that I was a witch – *ndiyathakatha* – and that I learnt witchcraft from my mother. So my husband could not stay with me any more.

The lawyer told me 'Your husband wants a divorce. He didn't give any specific reason but he said that he doesn't love you any more.' He told me that my husband had a letter from the third party insurance telling him that a large sum of money would be coming.

Then I swallowed my pride. I went back to that Guguletu house. I spoke to my husband and he told me that there was lots of money coming the following week. 'I want to eat it with my family, not with you and your children,' he said.

I said, 'Why, those are our children?'

'That's what my father and my brothers told me. I mustn't eat it with you. I'm going to come to New Crossroads tomorrow to collect the truck and to take the groceries which are in the shop because they were bought with my money.'

Then I said, 'That is not going to happen. I am not going to let you do that.'

The following morning he came with police vans and his family to collect the truck and the stock of groceries. I was helpless. My elderly parents were also helpless. They didn't know what to do. I had never before seen a man who had no mercy for his own children. I didn't even cry. I just gave him the keys to his truck and let them do whatever they wanted to do. My parents comforted me, telling me they were there for me. My children wouldn't suffer. I knew that. But the problem was that they were both pensioners. How long could they help me for? They were already old and their pension money was limited.

Since that time my husband has not even visited us. When he left my house, he was already out of the wheelchair and walking slowly. By 1985 he was walking all right again and he got married. He bought himself a house in Guguletu and after a year or so he sold that one. He bought a beautiful big house where he lives with his new wife.

BULELWA: We have not met with my father since the separation. We were not satisfied with how our mother explained it. We felt there was something else. Maybe my mother was not telling the truth. He didn't even come to our maternal grandmother's funeral in 1993. I don't miss him much because our mother works very hard for us.

On occasions Bulelwa expressed resentment about her father's new house, new wife and lack of support in spite of his material well-being. The pain of this neglect was excruciating for the children.

In spite of this traumatic family fracture, Bulelwa's mother worked hard to provide her children with a loving home and a good education. It was fortunate that her parents had earlier moved into a house in the same street not far from her own. The two households were run jointly after this trauma. They shared the joys and cares of life. Bulelwa spent most of her remaining childhood living in her grandparents' house, helping them with chores in their old age. They in turn gave support to their daughter and her children.

Bulelwa did well at school. When we met she was in Grade 9 at Guguletu Comprehensive School – at the time one of the few schools functioning well. She liked the teachers who encouraged her to work hard. They read, wrote and spoke English as part of the teachers' strategy to prepare them for life with English as the main language of communication. The school also offered computer skills training, encouraged debating forums and educational trips.

BULELWA: When our friends come they sit with us in the lounge and my mother lets us use her house freely. She would ask to be excused unless she doesn't know the friends. If she doesn't know them, we would introduce them. After we introduced them she would waste no time in making snacks and serving us.

Then she would go back to her bedroom. She told us that she understands the need for young people to have friends. She also had friends when she was growing up. She preferred boyfriends to girlfriends.

When it comes to friends my mother tries her best to satisfy us. If they come at night she prefers them to come inside the house. If they stand outside at night and send neighbouring children to call us she doesn't like it because she doesn't know whether they are our friends or strangers. She prefers that visitors should come in so that she can see who they are. There are many dangers at night. One can get hurt outside. It is best for our friends to come in. She says if friends do not want to come in, mothers become suspicious. Our friends know what our mother likes and dislikes.

My best friends are my sisters and cousins because where we stay there are fights over little things. My sisters and I decided to be our own best friends. We don't talk to any other children in our street. We do not know the reason for this estrangement. Other people come to try and ask us what is happening. Other children say we are putting ourselves above others because many of the things children in our street do, we don't do. We don't go to many of the places they go to. We do not smoke. We do not drink. So they have separated themselves from us. In fact we are not hurt, *asi hetsheki*, because at home we are many. We are four girls. So we are all friends. If one of us has a problem – like we do have teenage problems – we help one another to overcome those problems before we go to our mother.

Bulelwa's decision not to go outside the family was for her the best way of coping with her circumstances. Good peer relations and whatever support she could derive from such relationships had to be sacrificed. Success demanded that she distanced herself from the destructive lifestyles prevalent among her peers. The cost was alienation from her peers because success in places like New Crossroads, where the majority of people are unable to succeed, is seen as a threat to community solidarity.

The closeness between the Leseka sisters was not surprising. They realised how important it was to derive strength from one another in the face of a hostile neighbourhood and their mother's limited material and emotional resources.

Bulelwa's life came under increasing strain both at school and at home. The continual disruptions to schooling in the run-up to South Africa's first election in 1994 began to erode teaching and learning even in good schools like Guguletu Comprehensive High School.

As part of the project I arranged positions in schools outside the township for those among the group of sixteen who wanted to move.

Bulelwa and five others moved to Rhodes High in Mowbray at the beginning of 1994. Because it was connected to the train, bus and taxi routes it was accessible to township pupils.

Rhodes High was started in the 1940s as a traditional working-class school for white children. Like similar schools elsewhere in the country it opened its doors to all children in the early 1990s. The headmaster of the school was supportive of the new arrivals and did his best to ease their adjustment. But there was a huge gap between the New Crossroads pupils and their new peers. Their school experience had not prepared them for the discipline of regular classes and homework, the need for extra reading and self-motivation. Their reading, writing and mathematical skills were far below those expected of their age and class level. English was taken seriously as the medium of instruction unlike in township schools where teachers were often not competent users of the language. Bulelwa coped best of them all with the new challenges.

However, the stresses and strains of limited financial resources and single parenthood were taking their toll on Bulelwa's mother and she became subject to dramatic mood swings. On one occasion the sisters asked their mother for permission to go to a club in Guguletu. She had agreed. Come the day everyone completed their household chores early and prepared supper, then dressed up for their evening out. At that point Mrs Leseka asked the girls where they thought they were going. They reminded her and said she'd given them permission. Mrs Leseka refused to allow them out. The girls were furious. They stayed away for many hours simply roaming in the neighbourhood in frustration. The one sister, Fika, even branded her mother as cruel.

The next day Mrs Leseka locked herself in her bedroom and wouldn't talk to anyone. She did not even allow in her son, the youngest child, who usually shared the bedroom with her. He slept in Fika's bedroom that day.

After this incident Mrs Leseka did not speak to any of the children for a week. Bulelwa understood her mother's behaviour as frustration, describing her as a woman who found it hard to bear the burden of poverty and single parenthood. The only way of expressing this frustration was through anger and shutting everybody out.

By 1995 Bulelwa's family was in severe financial trouble. Bulelwa often found herself without money to get to school and was frequently absent. One of her teachers noted in her report that her frequent absenteeism was having a negative impact on her progress. The death of her grandmother in 1993 had deprived the family not only of a loved one, but also of an essential old-age pension which made a difference to the family's income.

Bulelwa managed to get a part-time job at the New Crossroads Youth Centre where she worked after school each day. The money was sufficient to cover her transport costs for the week and enabled her to attend school. The Youth Centre also gave her R50 as a once-off grant to buy books and a school uniform.

Then one afternoon she arrived at the Youth Centre in tears. She explained that she could not possibly justify keeping her money for school when there was no food in her home. Her mother was pressurising her to contribute this money to the household. Mrs Leseka had also being trying to persuade Bulelwa to transfer to Stembele Matiso High School in New Crossroads, which would solve the transport problem. Both knew that the education that Bulelwa would receive at the local high school was vastly inferior to that at Rhodes. But for Mrs Leseka, desperate to provide for her five children, this seemed a necessary sacrifice to enable the family to keep afloat.

Bulelwa knew all too well that a good education could be her only ticket out of the poverty of New Crossroads. Staying at a good school meant making a 'selfish' decision at the expense of her family's well-being, and against her mother's wishes. Not making this 'selfish' decision could cost her a brighter future. The long-term benefits of being in a better position to improve the family's welfare would also have to be foregone.

At the time a researcher on the project went to visit Mrs Leseka to talk to her about Bulelwa's dilemma, hoping to convince her of the importance of keeping Bulelwa at a good school. The researcher arrived to find that the Leseka's household furniture had just been taken away because Mrs Leseka had been unable to keep up the hire-purchase payments. The family had not only lost the furniture, but the total investment of the payments made up to that point. It was obviously not a good time to talk about Bulelwa's schooling. Bulelwa had to fight the battle alone.

41

In spite of all these obstacles, Bulelwa persevered. She read widely, had a good command of written and spoken English, planned ahead and worked diligently to achieve her goals. She was determined to make the best of life and her leadership qualities came into their own at different levels. She continued to work at the Youth Centre as part of our Child-to-Child programmes. She read to younger children. She told them stories which amused them and nurtured their curiosity. She in turn received financial and moral support from the Youth Centre. She also built on the Wilderness Leadership School trail experiences to promote an environmental awareness programme at the Youth Centre. The programme encouraged young people to explore the natural treasures in and around Cape Town. She became a volunteer of the Pride of Table Mountain project which took township youth onto the mountain every weekend.

Bulelwa graduated from high school at the end of 1996. In 1997 she obtained a commercial education diploma from Damelin correspondence college financed by a bursary from the Italian embassy which she had negotiated on her own. Her first job was at one of South Africa's largest insurance companies.

Bulelwa did not consider studying full time after high school graduation as it was too expensive. She also opted out of doing a university degree.

'There's a problem I see with going to university,' she told me. 'Studying for four years and then not being able to get a job and being stuck at home with a degree would be a risk. I don't want to spend a lot of money studying and then when it comes to searching for a job I face problems. I want to study while I work so that I can get experience.'

Bulelwa's personal life was also successful. She married in 1997 – a double wedding held in Port Elizabeth with one of her sister's marrying her husband's brother. A case of the sisters' solidarity stretching into their romantic lives.

III

One afternoon in 1997 Bulelwa floated into my home on the arm of her admiring husband. They looked gorgeous in their matching Afro outfits. Like a duet singing in harmony, they told me the story of their meeting, dating and finally marrying. 'The long and short of it is that Bulelwa was made for me,' said her husband. 'After watching her from a distance, one day I decided to talk to her. I asked her to describe the man of her dreams. After listening to her for a while I asked her if she has met anyone with the characteristics she had described. She said no. I then said that I am that person. That was the beginning of a mutual get-to-know-you process which was joined by my brother and her sister.'

Bulelwa and her husband have distanced themselves from what they perceive to be the destructive behaviour within the townships. They neither drink nor smoke. They are not interested in going to discos or clubs. When her husband, a commerce graduate of the University of the Western Cape, was offered an assignment as a model in a beer advertisement, he turned it down. Although the money was good, they decided it was unethical for him to promote a product of which they disapproved. Bulelwa spoke proudly of this incident and her husband who was unlike most of the other young men in New Crossroads.

She also spoke of the jealousy that other women in New Crossroads felt towards her and her sister. Both men were UWC graduates and had successful careers. Part of Bulelwa's explanation for having the wedding away from Cape Town was that having the ceremony in New Crossroads might have been dangerous.

'I didn't want a white wedding because people here are very cruel,' she told me. 'There's a lot of jealousy. My sister and I are married to brothers who are coveted by all the girls. We would have got ourselves into danger if we had opted for a big white wedding.'

The decision not to have an ostentatious wedding was also influenced to some extent by the expense it would have involved. Such weddings require a minimum outlay of R20 000 – not a viable proposition for a family with no regular source of income.

Bulelwa's success had boosted her self-confidence. But there was a fragility that occasionally broke through in her tendency to talk about her achievements. She made sure you knew about all the things that she had accomplished and felt proud of. For instance, when she was being interviewed about her last years in high school she rattled off a list of things she had been involved in. She then paused and watched that they were being noted down, adding, 'Make sure you do not forget that I was a prefect.' She also made it known that not only had she coped academically at a 'white' school, but had also been actively involved in school life as the founder of an environmental organisation. This tendency continued into her adult life and initially I was a bit taken aback. I remember a casual telephone conversation where she gave me her husband's cellphone number and perhaps too gloatingly said, 'It's going to be my phone soon.'

Of course these statements are about pride and self-affirmation. Bulelwa continually had to remind herself of how far she had come given her socioeconomic background and compared to those around her. It was part of her way of motivating herself to continue succeeding in an environment in which envy and resentment of successful people could sap one's energy.

Bulelwa had thought about visiting her father. Since her marriage his family had started taking an interest in her. It might have been that now that she was financially independent her father felt free to relate to her without fearing that she would make demands on his material resources. Interestingly, Bulelwa's younger brother was close to his father. In Bulelwa's view this relationship was not surprising – he was an only son, and sons are valued more by their fathers than are the daughters. Perhaps, too, her brother was too young at the time of their father's desertion to have experienced the pain that upset the rest of the family.

Bulelwa fluctuated between anger and suspicion against her father and his family, yet believed that as members of the same family they should resolve their differences. It was a difficult tension to sort out.

CHAPTER THREE

Bulelani
Teach me how to be a man

I

My second success story concerns Bulelani, an extraordinary person, remarkably tall with a calm, powerful presence. His maturity was striking and he approached all issues – ordinary and extraordinary – in a serious philosophical manner. Bulelani's ideas differed significantly from those of other young people in all the encounters I had with him. His wisdom and warmth were striking in one so young.

Bulelwa noted that Bulelani was highly respected in New Crossroads by both young and old. He recognised this respect but approached it philosophically. Respect was something that needed to be earned. Bulelani believed that if you offered respect to another person, the offer would be made in return.

'One needs to give respect in order to get it,' he told me. 'I respect guys – I give them a place. If I meet a small guy I try to be small. If I meet an old guy I try to be old – be on their same level, respect them.'

II

Bulelani was, in a sense, a miracle. In 1979, at the age of two and a half years he was run over by a car and sustained serious head injuries which left him unconscious for some time. When he was discharged from hospital his mother, Ms Mbuli (who had lost the father of her son in a car accident shortly after Bulelani's birth), was told that her son would not be able to attend a normal school on account of the brain damage.

A few years later, shortly after he had started primary school, Bulelani was involved in yet another car accident. This time his skull was fractured. Most people, including his mother, did not expect him to survive.

As she put it shortly after we met, 'That time I said, "Now he won't make it." But miracles do happen. There he is. Although he had problems at school he was a normal child. The only thing that I noticed about him after the accident was that he was sensitive and emotional. And you will notice when Bulelani walks you will hear crrcrr – the bones creaking. At the time of the first accident he had broken bones, but because he was a child he was lucky because he was still growing and his bones were soft. But now it's fixed. He even plays sports. When you go out camping with him you will hear the noise of his bones, but don't worry about it. He is now fine.'

Bulelani bore the marks of his accidents, one of which was a visible dent on his forehead where a metal plate was inserted to protect the brain after the skull fracture. This dent, combined with his height, made him stand out wherever he was.

Despite the accidents, Bulelani did remarkably well both at school and at a local technikon where he studied and successfully completed mechanical engineering in 1998.

Bulelani was brought up by his mother, and they had a close though complex relationship.

She was at school in the Transkei when she became pregnant with Bulelani, dropped out, then, with the sudden death of his father, was forced to move to Cape Town to live with her mother and her three brothers. This created tensions.

'When I looked at the behaviour of my brothers I decided that I would not take it any more,' she told me. 'It was really bad. They had girlfriends sleeping with them in front of my mother and these girlfriends had children. I decided to look for a house.'

In 1985 Ms Mbuli moved with Bulelani and her second child, Vusi, to her own house in New Crossroads. Vusi was two years younger than Bulelani. Ms Mbuli never married and Bulelani mentioned on several occasions that he did not like his mother bringing boyfriends home. Understandably he resented the small family space being invaded by outsiders, particularly when he was so close to his mother, and jealous of her affections. It was also understandable that his mother should want to, and be able to, also have friends. Ironically, Bulelani was proud that he had always been allowed to bring friends into his home.

During the project, whenever I talked to him he always spoke lovingly of his mother. She was a strong woman who had managed to raise both Bulelani and his younger brother under extraordinarily difficult conditions. She had studied privately and graduated from high school. She worked as a salesperson at a furniture shop and augmented her income with part-time acting in serialised radio dramas. In 1991, through sheer determination, she got Bulelani into Rhodes High School.

MS MBULI: I just could see from the unending school boycotts and the violence in the area that my son's future was not going to come to anything unless I did something about his schooling. But I had no money to take him to schools outside of the townships. I had been told about Rhodes High by friends who also said that the headmaster was a good and kind man. I decided to approach him. I told him about the problems of township schools and asked that he take my son. When he agreed, I also told him that I was not working at the time and had no money for the required school uniform. He agreed that he could use his old school uniform until I could afford a new one. Then came the most difficult part. I said that I also did not have money for his bus fare or his lunch. He looked at me and then said, 'Bring your son here and I will do what I can.' I felt like hugging him. I was so grateful.

For a number of months Bulelani wore his undersized 'out of place' school uniform, shared his headmaster's lunch and was given bus fare by the school. A strong bond developed between pupil and headmaster. When his mother got a new job she paid her debts.

The loss of his father weighed heavily on Bulelani and he maintained contact with his father's family in the Transkei. The loss of a father always complicates the lives of children, but it is a particular handicap in a community where the father is the key to entry into the world of men. For instance, it is the father who provides the name and introduces the boy to ancestors in a ritual called *imbeleko*.

This ritual is performed a few months after birth. A goat is slaughtered, traditional beer brewed, food and drink offered to both the living and the dead. The inclusion of ancestors in the ritual is to cement the ties of the clan. Everyone – family and neighbours – join to witness the entry of a new member into the corporate whole.

An elder of the family on the paternal side formally summons the ancestors by pouring beer on the ground in the family courtyard and sprinkling snuff. He uses the family *isiduko* (clan name which is used to praise members of the lineage) to implore them to shower their blessings on the child, and to ensure that her/his future is under their protection. Those assembled add their voices. The child is welcomed as a joint responsibility by the nuclear and extended family as well as the neighbours who join the celebrations.

Difficulties arise when children are born out of wedlock. In cases involving parents who are on reasonably good terms even though not married, the child is still acknowledged as part of his father's lineage, and the *imbeleko* is conducted accordingly. Otherwise the child is introduced to her/his maternal ancestral lineage, assumes their surname, and *isiduko*. The child becomes the responsibility of his/her mother's brothers, one of whom, usually the eldest, is charged with the principal obligations of watching over the child for its entire life.

Failure to perform the *imbeleko* ritual is believed to make the child, and later adult, vulnerable to misfortune. After all, if your ancestors have not been properly informed about your arrival how would they be able to spread their protective wings around you? Many young adults who find themselves facing multiple setbacks are often asked to check with their parents as to whether their misfortune is not related to neglect of the *imbeleko* ritual. Should that be the case, the family often arranges a belated ceremony. It is never too late to make amends with your ancestors. They have long memories and infinite patience. They are only too familiar with the failings of human beings.

Bulelani has had to rely on his mother's brothers to stand in for his father on ceremonial occasions such as these. However, urbanisation, which scatters families, and limited material resources restricted his uncles' abilities to be meaningful substitute fathers.

Consequently Bulelani's mother brought her sons up single-handedly and expected both boys to share domestic chores. Bulelani spent Saturday mornings cleaning the house and doing his own laundry. He could cook simple meals. He was a hard worker who had set his sights high. He studied regularly every day including Saturday afternoons. His home was always neat and exuded warmth.

It was important for me to remember that as a boy in the mid-1980s he saw the battles between the 'fathers' and the 'comrades' that caused mayhem in the townships and squatter settlements. During those battles young males, some barely in their teens, were forced to do battle against the 'fathers' who were regarded as controlling the squatter camps with the support of the police. The 'fathers' identified themselves in battle by wearing white head-dresses which earned them the Afrikaans name 'witdoeke'.

In the battle for territorial control that constituted this phase of 'the struggle' fellow residents maimed and killed one another. Warlords violently carved out territories over which they could exercise absolute control and extract 'taxes' for their own pockets. The police unsurprisingly sided with this conservative faction to drive deep wedges into a community that had, up to then, successfully resisted some of the impositions against Africans in the Western Cape. Battle lines were not just drawn along politically correct positions, but also along what constituted a 'man'. 'Comrade' became the catch phrase, the password into 'manhood' – the social leveller between 'men' and 'boys'.

With the blurring of divisions between men and boys came role reversals and ambiguities. Young 'comrades' presiding over 'people's courts' between 1985 and 1988 publicly flogged errant male heads of households who were reported by their wives or children to have been neglectful or abusive. When asked how they felt about their sons flogging their own 'fathers', one woman said, 'What is worse, letting children handle corpses and preside over funerals, or getting them to settle family disputes? There are no longer taboos against anything – once you let children come into the presence of the dead you can't stop them from anything else.'

With characteristic insight Bulelani said of this period: 'It was difficult to grow up as a black child because you saw things you should not see and you heard things you should not hear. Language is also part of violence. Adults often used rude language that hurt us. I remember seeing dead bodies with their insides lying next to them. You knew what a policeman looked like [a reference to the then predominately white police force]. A white child doesn't grow up under such conditions.'

When Bulelani's mother and her family moved to New Crossroads in 1982, they were battle-weary and impatient with the never-ending demands of warlords who extracted heavy levies from all households to finance their reigns of terror. The battle for access to urban resources had become a battle to enrich the warlords and their loyal followers. What had begun as a struggle for justice had become a vehicle of further injustice.

'Comrades' who had become used to the power they wielded in the battles for control in Old Crossroads had to find a new form of expression in New Crossroads. The violent way disputes were settled became embedded in peer relations. Gang activity attained new heights. Young people involved in these criminal activities were referred to as *comtsotsis* to indicate their tenuous relationship with 'comrades' in the struggle.

At the age of eleven, Bulelani was forced to become a member of a gang.

BULELANI: The reason why I became a member of a gang is that one day I came home from the dentist via Nyanga taxi rank. I was called by a group of five boys. They asked me where I stayed. I said New Crossroads. I had no way of anticipating problems with them. I could see from their faces that they were people with no respect for anybody. One started to kick me. Another said I was the person they were looking for. When I asked what was happening, they said, 'You dare to ask?' I had to defend myself against a knife. I managed to run towards some houses.

I was very angry and in great pain because I had just been to the dentist. I did not ask or think twice. I just took off my clothes and put on some funny ones and went out into the street. I hate to carry a knife, but I am very good at throwing a brick. I had to be on the side of the Badboys [a gang] because they were from New Crossroads. Because of what happened to me, I decided to help them. I hated Nyanga East gangs from that day onwards.

I have seen innocent people stabbed, but I did not stab anyone – I didn't carry a knife, the only thing I used was a brick.

During the period 1987-1988 the Civic Association and the residents of New Crossroads tried to stop gang activity in their neighbourhoods.

Parents of children involved in gangs were warned not to let those children back into their homes or they would be evicted from the township. Parents were ordered to give neither food nor accommodation to their gangster children as part of the campaign. Mothers had to withdraw from nurturing their errant male children – violent behaviour had to be met with further violence. The rallying cry was *Kwavukwa, umtshayelo nenkwenkwe* – Wake up, a broom must meet a boy. Adult men were literally being called on to clear boys off the streets with broomsticks or any object that could inflict pain. No boys were allowed to be on the streets after nine o'clock at night.

BULELANI: The Comrades also joined the fray – they hunted down the Badboys and beat them. There was war between the Comrades and the Badboys for a long time. The residents of New Crossroads told themselves that they were going to fight – boys were not going to be allowed to rule New Crossroads. The adults ultimately won.

The clearing of the streets by adults was an important symbolic statement about their unwillingness to let chaos reign. They had to take back the neighbourhood so that community relations that had been fractured by gang activity could be restored.

Bulelani handled a difficult place and time with great ingenuity and a sense of humour. He told me how he managed to convince his peers that his move to Rhodes High was not in any way a reflection of his weakening commitment to 'the struggle'. There was general agreement among his peers that most teachers in the township schools were not equal to the task. He suggested to them that by going to a better school he would become a resource for them by tutoring them over weekends. He laughed as he told the story – yet at the time being necklaced to death as a sell-out was a very real threat.

Bulelani was consistent in his criticism of school boycotts that became part of the anti-apartheid struggle tactics from 1976 to the 1990s. Although other children in the project expressed concern about some of the negative side-effects of boycotts, Bulelani was the only one who was consistently and strongly critical about their inherent value in the wider scheme of things.

BULELANI: These school boycotts didn't only mean boycotting school, but other people's lives were threatened because cars were stoned. Children involved in such action enjoyed this. Some took food from vans. A poor person would go to a wholesale depot to buy things to sell in his shop and he would meet with a group of students who would take everything out of his van. They were not going to sell those things to buy the books they were crying about. They would eat those things and sell them to buy cigarettes. They wouldn't go and study when the schools were temporarily shut. They would stand on every street corner in mobs until late.

Their parents didn't know what was happening during boycotts. One parent was at work when she received a telephone call informing her that her son was in jail because of throwing stones at a police van. This was difficult for a poor mother because she must try to get money to pay bail for her son.

If we could examine these things carefully and the way in which they affected our parents, we would know that boycotting was not good. We have seen people on television striking at factories and then some of the people lose their jobs and the little money they earn. We must learn to identify problems and address them properly. We must go to school and to work rather than sitting down and saying, 'tools down or pens down.' At that stage of our development we really needed education. South Africa needs us with our education. We need to be good examples.

Bulelani's views were unpopular in 1993. They indicated a pragmatism that was rooted in the everyday reality of struggle. They also reflected the visionary in Bulelani. Sacrificing your education was a cost too high to pay for broader political goals, particularly when you could not at that stage envision fundamental change in the foreseeable future. Bulelani had seen too many students who had given up on the system because they felt they had nothing to lose. In his opinion education was the only way he could possibly get ahead. He was also not impressed with the argument that one could not make progress at school because there were not enough textbooks.

As he said to me, 'You can study without textbooks. You must use the teachers' notes. People don't see that time is important. I know, because I went to school at Andile Primary. I passed without textbooks. The other thing that I see is that there is no respect among schoolchildren. They do not respect their teachers. They come to class when the teacher is already teaching. Some make a noise. Some are busy smoking. Most of the teachers decide to leave the class because nobody shows any respect for them. So this thing of boycotting is something that people do for fun. Although there are good reasons to be angry, boycotting is not the answer.'

Bulelani's school career was not all plain sailing. Among its many difficult patches was a physical fight with a fellow student at Rhodes High. This was a white boy from a poor working-class background whom Bulelani accused of racism. The headmaster diffused the tension by getting both boys into his car and driving around the Cape Peninsula threatening not to stop the car until they had sorted out their problem. The headmaster pointed out the similarities of their family circumstances and the need for emotional control even when provoked. Both boys were relieved when he stopped for lunch at a fast-food restaurant and gave them a treat. They may not have become the best of friends after that episode but they developed empathy for each other.

Bulelani was often frustrated by the slow progress he made in mastering science and mathematics – a legacy of poor foundations laid by apartheid education, although it might also have had something to do with the two head injuries he suffered. He also worried about his body which he described in uncomplimentary terms. He saw himself as being too tall. He resented the dent on his forehead. At times his determination to succeed seemed almost self-destructive.

For example, one day Bulelani's mother arrived at his school in tears because he had been angry and frustrated about his schoolwork. During his fits of anger he threw books around the house and bashed his head against the wall. His mother's concern only served to distress him further. He was also seen at school bashing his head against a wall and complaining that he could not get things into his head quickly enough.

Bulelani did not only direct his anger at himself. On a wilderness trail he was described as 'venting manipulative anger and power over the younger children' by one of my colleagues. She felt that Bulelani was 'full of aspirations and bitter about his current position.' When he admonished his peers for not expressing gratitude to the organisers of the trail, he was cautioned by my colleague that his behaviour toward his peers was inappropriate. He became extremely angry. For the rest of that day he refused to let anyone near him. He would not talk to anyone. He walked ahead of the entire party on his own.

One of Bulelani's school reports described him as being in the high honours class at school and doing well academically. But it noted that he was having trouble controlling his emotions. Bulelani had a strong sense of responsibility to himself, his family, and his community – some regarded it as overdeveloped and difficult to bear.

During a workshop Bulelani tried to explain his friendships with people in New Crossroads and his ambivalence about his relationships with people. At one level he enjoyed being with people, at another, he felt there was a frustrating, ever-present burden which they couldn't ease. Sometimes it was preferable for him to be alone with his feelings.

BULELANI: I don't trust anyone on this earth. Most of the time I want to be alone. I am not happy. I don't go to anyone when I have a problem because I can't identify what my problem is. I don't seem to like anything I do. I don't know how to describe this but I am not happy at all. Even when I am with friends I am happy for a short time but I will start again so I really don't know what my problem is. I like having friends but they don't help me with anything. So I don't think I'm happy at all. That is why I like to be alone.

In 1994, as part of a school assignment, he wrote a poem which yet again expressed his loneliness and yearning.

> My Love
> Me ...
> I smile with Love,
> I see with Love,
> I dance with Love,
> I wish with Love,
> No wonder why I'm in Love.

Yes I walk with Love,
Socialise with Love,
Confused with Love,
And wonder when I'm falling in Love.

To me flowers mean Love,
The sea, the morning and night,
They all mean Love.

I speak about Love,
Talk with Love,
And give with Love,
But when am I going to receive Love?

For Bulelani life was a continual struggle between a sense of optimism and determination to succeed, and the frustration of not being able to attain the goals he set for himself. A caring, responsible, mature young man wrestling with the child within. He was struggling to come to terms with the limitations of his environment as well as those of his own abilities in a desperate struggle that at times threatened to overwhelm him. But he did not give up.

Nor did he give up on his community. Gang warfare was a recurring theme in New Crossroads. Bulelani worried a great deal about the effects of this warfare on the young. In 1997 several young boys from New Crossroads were involved in shootings. Bulelani took the violence very seriously. He tried to come up with ideas about how he, as an individual and a member of the community, could positively intervene and do something about the situation. His attitude was unusual as most of the other people I spoke to about township violence regarded it as an unfortunate but fairly hopeless situation. Bulelani, on the other hand, was certain that something could be done about it.

'Last year they were also getting out of hand – that's why we were calling on them all the time. I knew this was going to happen. We could have prevented it but we weren't there for them then,' he lamented to me. 'They did not feel the support of the community. I will convince them – I haven't yet lost hope.'

Bulelani was an idealist. He recognised the boys involved in this violence as part of his community. He regarded them as young people like himself. At the time he said to me: 'I know these boys – they're sweet boys when they're sober. Two thirds of them are dead already. Some of them I know. It's not nice to see small boys dead. I have a dream that the youth who are violent will come back to humanity. Life for them is getting out of hand – if we don't act now there will be problems. Gangsterism is not a situation we can live with – this has been proved. They're not the first teenagers to get involved with gangsterism. It's been proved that you can't live with it. Once you kill one then you kill more.'

III

Bulelani's determination to make something of himself extended to searching for traditional support on his journey into manhood. He embraced the Xhosa initiation ritual through circumcision. He went into traditional initiation with a group of thirty-two other young men during the December 1996 vacation. They were transported to a remote mountainous area in the Franschhoek district about sixty kilometres from New Crossroads.

His mother's brother stood in for his late father as is the tradition in these matters.

BULELANI: Our parents sat around and discussed my readiness to undergo initiation. I do not have a father so my uncle represented me. It was all controlled by the parents. Even when I came back I was still under parental guidance.

When you get out there everything goes to the dark side. It is a difficult process. If you have no discipline you cannot live – you die. It is far from home and harsh. You are forced back to where you come from – to the same Being who gathered you together – Morena or Nkosi, God.

There was a lot of competition among us. One of the guys had to be the leader, *sosuthu*, and people fight to lead. I was to be one of the leaders but held back when I saw the competition.

Being initiated into manhood is about responsibility, it's about discipline, it's about being respectful. You get to know that even an eight-year-old is a person, you should respect that. You grow not from going through initiation per se, but from becoming more mature.

Many adult males speak of the toughness of the traditional initiation. In his autobiography, *A Long Walk to Freedom*, Nelson Mandela recalled the pain and anxiety of his own initiation. He, too, had to get through initiation without the support of his father who had already died. He too had to had to rely on uncles for support.

Initiation is a ritual based on the importance of instilling discipline and fortitude in the face of physical pain and emotional strain. But it is also an opportunity for older men to teach the young how to be real men. The ritual is ideally conducted with young men of eighteen years or older. They are regarded as both physically and emotionally mature enough to both endure and benefit from the experience.

As an initiate Bulelani would have had to build himself a temporary home with reeds, grass and any other available disposable material, an *ibhoma*. The reason his group were taken to the Franschhoek mountains was to distance them from the routines of daily life.

The night before the actual 'going to the bush' there is a preparatory ceremony which is held in the *ubuhlanti*, cattle kraal. In the urban areas a ritual space is created in the backyard of the initiate's home which is declared out of bounds for women for the duration of the ceremony. A goat is slaughtered and cooked to provide meat for the initiate and those accompanying him on his journey. He is given a whole forequarter of the goat to eat in preparation for the strict diet that follows. Much beer and brandy flows and is enjoyed by the men during an all-night ceremony. At about midnight Bulelani would have been fed *umphokoqo namasi*, rich sour milk and specially cooked mealie meal porridge, his last proper meal for many days to come.

At dawn the young man is led – nay chased – to the nearest river where he takes a cold bath from which he emerges to face the *ingcibi*'s, the surgeon's, sharp knife which parts him forever from his prepuce. The purpose of the cold bath is to constrict the blood vessels and minimise blood loss. The initiate has to shout without flinching at the pain searing through his body: *Ndiyindoda!* – I am a man. It is regarded as a great embarrassment to the family and the initiate for him to show any sign of wincing.

The *ikhankatha*, the equivalent of a male nurse as well as a counsellor, then takes over the care of the initiate who is led to his new abode. He occupies his *ibhoma* until he is healed and ready to re-enter the world as a new man. The *ikhankatha* sees to the dressings, the discipline of not taking fluids during the first week until there is enough healing of the wound to permit easy passage of urine. The first week's diet consists of only partially cooked dried mielies.

Much attention is given to healing the wound. It is dressed frequently to ensure cleanliness, it is treated with natural herbs, and the initiate is kept naked except for a blanket wrapped around his body which allows enough airing of the genital area. White clay is smeared over the naked body to protect the skin from the elements, including ultraviolet light. Encouragement and wise counsel comes from the *ikhankatha* leading to a strong bond between the young man and his older minder. Other men come and go to add their support and encouragement. This is the most important aspect of teaching young people to become men and promote male bonding.

As soon as the *ikhankatha* sees signs of healing he informs the family through the male head of the household of the readiness of the young man to be served meat, *ukojiswa*. A sheep is slaughtered in the bush and the young man given a forequarter to devour to make up for the week of near starvation and to replace his iron stores. From then onwards the initiate is permitted to eat what he pleases.

Feeding initiates is a huge responsibility. Preparation of the food is assigned to a young girl. Traditionally this role fell on a virgin, or where that's not possible, someone who has to abstain from sexual intercourse throughout the period until the initiate returned home. It is believed that any engagement in sexual activity by such a person would endanger the life of the initiate. This taboo is a great way of focussing the mind of the cook on her responsibilities without the distractions of romantic affairs.

A group of young boys, *amangcalatha*, usually chosen from among members of the extended family, is assigned the responsibility of seeing to the comfort of the initiate. They make his fire, fetch his food from the cook, guard him and alert the elders of any untoward occurrence. They literally stay at his side physically and emotionally until he returns to normal life. At the end of the ceremony they are rewarded with the clothing the new man casts off as 'boys' clothes'. The *ikhankatha* has the sole discretion over the right time to 'come out'. When he is satisfied with the degree of healing he consults with male members of the family to set the date for the homecoming. The women are notified to start preparing for the celebration. Home-made beer is brewed, sheep are slaughtered, lots of liquor is bought, including brandy for each of the main players: the *ingcibi*, the *ikhankatha*, and all the men who played various roles. The women too share in the ceremony.

The morning Bulelani returned would have been a day of great joy. Just like the first day of initiation, no one would have slept the night before he returned. There would be much singing and dancing fuelled by a liberal flow of alcohol. At the *ibhoma* much the same celebration would go on until dawn. His *ibhoma* would then have been set alight with its contents, signalling the end of his boyhood and the begin-ning of his manhood when the *umkhwetha*, initiate, becomes an *ikrwa-la*, a new man. Bulelani would not have looked back once the *ibhoma* was set on fire; his gaze had to be directed at the future.

Now the initiate has to walk with his eyes fixed in the direction of the river where he is to wash, be smeared with red ochre, wrapped in a new blanket and led back to his home with much singing and dancing.

The women then join in welcoming the new man by ululating and dancing. The young man is led back to *ebuhlanti*, the ritual space in the backyard, where he is set before the men of the village or town-ship. The *ikhankatha* testifies that this young man has fulfilled the obligations to be accepted into the ranks of manhood. After much corroboration by those who participated in one way or another in the ritual and praise for the young man's discipline and bravery, the festivities start. The young man is then led into a room in his home in which he is to remain under the care of young girls from his ex-tended family. A long queue of people files in throughout the day to welcome him, counsel him and give him presents. His family provide the new clothes into which he is allowed to change. He has to con-tinue to apply red ochre to his body for a week or two.

The male initiation ritual has become an expensive affair. The mixture of old traditions with new ones has added to the costs. For example, the custom of discarding all the clothes worn before initiation made sense when there was a clear distinction between boys' and men's clothes. The traditional loin-cloth designed for boys had to be abandoned for more appropriately designed outfits. In the contemporary context a slavish following of 'tradition' entails discarding the expensive fashion clothing which today's teenagers wear and buying new outfits including khaki pants, long-sleeved, dark-coloured shirts, smart jacket, shoes, underwear, and a hat prescribed for the first few weeks of the new man's life. This costs a lot of money. As does new bedlinen and other required items.

The feast is also expensive. Several sheep and a liquor supply of home brew, many cases of beer, wine, and brandy runs into hundreds if not thousands of rands. Poor families struggle to find the means to afford this ritual and may end up in debt trying to meet the high expectations of their sons while conforming to new demands.

Women are also given space in this male ritual. The women led by the mother of the young man – *izibazana* – are given a chance later in the day to celebrate with him and present him with gifts. The old and new mix comfortably as the women sing – each holding two bottles of brandy to symbolise the breasts which fed the young man as a baby and that now produce alcohol to celebrate his manhood. It is a moving moment for mother and son who see each other for the first time after his weeks spent in the bush.

Unfortunately for the families where things went wrong and the initiate died, this turns into a day of mourning. In the past the women would not have been told of the demise of their son until the end of the initiation period. A clay pot, traditionally the vessel used by the young boys to take the initiate's food to the *ibhoma*, would be ritually broken at the gate to signal the death.

Sadly many young men have died needlessly over the last few years because of lack of attention by those responsible for them. Commercialisation of the initiation ritual has also led to many irresponsible people luring young men without their parents' consent into botched circumcision rituals. There is also the hardship suffered by those from poor families who get little support from neighbours in the absence of fathers or responsible male relatives. The ritual becomes a long, lonely process.

These factors have unfortunately begun to discredit what is an important part of the culture of indigenous African people. Much is being done in some parts of South Africa to improve the safety levels to ensure this age-old ritual continues. Partnerships between traditional healers and medical practitioners are improving safety levels in parts of the Eastern Province. The HIV/Aids epidemic has put new urgency into properly sterilising circumcision tools as well as paying attention to the dressing process. The traditional use of one spear to circumcise a whole group of young men has no place in today's highly risky environment.

IV

Bulelani went through this ritual successfully. His disciplined approach to life as well as the support he derived from his mother's brothers helped him, and taught him how to be a man in traditional Xhosa custom.

A final detail about Bulelani that sticks in my mind was a wish he articulated in one of our discussions: 'I want to be prosperous in my studies and want some of the people I've grown up with to see life in the same way I do. Not that they should necessarily have the same perspective, but that they must want to achieve. I want to see everyone prosperous and living a life they enjoy. I feel that the spirit of youth here has diminished. Eventually I want to go to the University of Cape Town to do Masters. I want to be highly qualified.'

CHAPTER FOUR

Family

Induku ayinamzi – The rod destroys homes

I

I soon came to realise that the majority of children in New Cross-roads had not had the good fortune of having their mothers at their beck and call. Among the sixteen adolescents in my project there was a disturbing pattern of discontinuity with their mothers. Only seven of them had stayed with their mothers into their late teenage years. One had to forego the intimate relationship with his mother at the age of twelve. Five had their time with their mothers interrupted in early childhood, never to be restored again. Two were abandoned after birth and brought up by relatives, although one had regular contact with his mother. Single female-headed households are very common in this township even though the idea of the family is heavily influenced by patriarchal values.

During the project I heard many heart-rending personal stories. There was Pule who felt abandoned. She was cared for by her grandmother and her mother's sister after her mother left to work in Johannesburg. She was an insecure youngster with an eagerness to please and be embraced, attentive to her friends and those around her. She was attractive with a set of uneven shining white teeth. When I met her, her late-adolescent body was still struggling to find a healthy balance between muscle and fat. She saw little of her mother and resented being abandoned. In many ways she had been adopted into her aunt's family, although there were still expectations that her mother should ultimately take financial responsibility for her. So when Pule's cousins got new clothes, she was left out and felt sad. She found it difficult understanding how her mother could be absent from her life both physically and materially, and had been disappointed many times by her mother's failure to keep promises.

PULE: My mum and I don't communicate well. She is always bankrupt when I ask her for financial assistance. I once went to Gauteng to visit her but she did not give me new clothes nor money nor anything like the other kids. I've told myself that when I'm well educated and have a good job I won't support my mum because she didn't support me.

Although her grandmother offered some sort of emotional support, the fact that Pule was financially not part of her aunt's family hurt her. She was less well off than her cousins – a major source of pain for this young woman. To live with the knowledge that your own mother has abandoned you undermines your sense of worth.

I came across many similar examples of complex family relationships during the project. Children were often partially adopted into an extended family, but not afforded the same level of resources offered to the 'real' family members. Although the adopting family accepted the presence of the child, it became hard pressed by the scarcity of resources, both emotional and financial. It was only natural that when it came to allocating scarce resources your own offspring would get priority. Doing the right thing was not easy.

There were many instances where the distinction between kin and non-kin was blurred by necessity. Lolo's was one. She carried her poverty with dignity. I first met her when she was twelve years old but remember her as a young teenager with an innocent baby face smeared with thick layers of petroleum jelly. Her clothes were clean and neat but worn. She was shy and lacked the self-confidence to start conversations with her peers.

Her mother had walked out on her alcoholic husband and moved to Mossel Bay to live with a boyfriend. Lolo always insisted that her mother had only gone to Mossel Bay to promote her business of selling sheep's heads and would return some day. She continued living with her father, six brothers (one was stabbed to death when Lolo was fourteen) and two sisters in a house with two bedrooms, a kitchen and a living room.

Lolo was brought up by her father's sister from the age of two until she was eight years old and regarded her as her mother. She had come to Cape Town to join her parents in 1988 and only then got to know them. She said of her mother: 'I did not know that she was my mother. I called my *dadobawo* [her father's sister, i.e. her aunt] mama, and my mother, *dadobawo*. My heart was sore, because my mother said: 'That's not your mother. She's your father's sister. I gave birth to you.'

During the time with her alcoholic father Lolo came to draw support and comfort from Sisi Makoti (which translates as sister newly married woman), the wife of a lodger who had become part of the family. In fact she became the housekeeper and primary caregiver to the large 'family' of thirteen people including her own three children and husband. They exchanged rooms with Lolo's eldest sister who moved into the leaking shack in the backyard so that they could have one of the two bedrooms that would be safer for the young children. Sisi Makoti was touched by this generosity and regarded Lolo's elder sister as a sister. Their relationship was mutually beneficial at both a personal and family level as Sisi Makoti reduced Lolo's sister's responsibility of being the head of the household by giving emotional support as well as financial support which came from her husband's income. These two women organised the family's monthly budget of R400, half of this literally being taken from the pockets of the alcoholic father. Despite the women's efforts, however, the home was untidy and often lacked basic necessities.

The diet was limited to a mixture of samp and beans with little variation throughout the month. Bread was only affordable when the wages came in.

Sisi Makoti talked of the frustration of not being able to keep a slice of this rare bread for her toddler without someone else snatching it. She said that she was often tempted to hide food to preserve it for the young ones, but didn't, feeling this would be a sin.

Lolo relied on Sisi Makoti and her eldest sister to protect her from her alcoholic father with whom she shared a bedroom together with her two younger sisters. The father often became abusive physically and verbally. Mercifully, as the years progressed he seemed to retreat into an alcoholic haze and his violence ceased. He still contributed to the family budget.

The meaning of family in this context was fluid. Sisi Makoti – a total stranger – had to all intents and purposes become a member of Lolo's family. She shared the home, the joys and pains. When Lolo's brother was murdered their mother attended the funeral but behaved like an outsider, contributing nothing to the funeral expenses nor staying afterwards to mourn with the family as is the custom. Lolo was confused and pained by her mother's behaviour.

II

To reiterate: more than half the children in the project hadn't experienced the continuity of maternal care that most of us take for granted. During our discussions it became patently clear that this was a common occurrence for children in this community. Often mothers had to separate from their children because of the migrant labour system which forced many women to live fractured lives divided between their rural homes and their husband's places in Cape Town. These places often prevented family life. For instance, many parents of the young people in our research lived in single-sex migrant men's hostels where their mothers were 'illegals' subject to arrest on sight.

The migrant labour system expected African women to divide themselves into faithful wives who ran the rural household and mothers who nurtured the children that would become the economy's unskilled labour force. For eleven months of the year these women were to lead celibate lives and focus on mothering the children. Little consideration went into the difficulty of re-establishing intimacy between husband and wife after such a long separation. Suspicions of adulterous activities poisoned many relationships. Often innocent women were physically and sexually abused by jealous husbands. Tension could flare up during the month's visit as the man tried to re-establish his authority in the household.

Many men ended up with two families: an urban woman to satisfy immediate sexual needs; a rural wife to keep the home stable. Given low wages men were trapped into neglecting their rural families. Consequently from the 1970s onwards, many women increasingly braved the threat of arrest under influx-control regulations to join their husbands in urban areas even if it meant leaving their children with relatives. Saving their marriages was seen as a long-term insurance policy for themselves and their children. In the short term children had to do without motherly love.

The squatter areas absorbed most of the incoming rural families, yet they were unsafe during the civil war that lasted from the mid-1980s until the election in 1994. Despite the squalor of the squatter camps women tried to create the warmth and intimacy of family life inside their hardboard and tin shacks, or sent their children back to relatives in the rural areas.

Given the dictates of poverty, single parents often faced an awful choice: to ensure the physical survival of their children at the expense of emotional nourishment. It is a Hobson's choice imposed by a society that has failed to support family life. Pule and Lolo were just two of its victims.

There were also children who fell foul of the rituals and customs of the strong patriarchal Xhosa culture of this community and their kin in the Eastern Cape. The *imbeleko* ritual places limitations on the movement of children between families. A child born before marriage is expected to stay in his/her mother's family. Even if the mother gets married later on, the child is to remain behind in her natal home. Traditional practices such as these are intended to create harmony within families but have become sources of fragmentation. Too many children are born out of wedlock to sustain this practice. Too many marriages end in divorce and it is unrealistic expecting women to sacrifice their children in pursuit of elusive wedded bliss.

It is difficult assessing the long-term impact of 'abandonment' on children. Dumo, one of the adolescents I got to know during the project, had to part from his mother for the first time when he was twelve years old.

He'd lived with her in Old Crossroads until she went to live with her new husband in Paarl. As he told me, 'In our family a woman has to leave her children born before marriage if she marries a different man from the father of her children. I was told that I belonged here, and had to stay whilst she joins her new family.'

Dumo's mother's brother, to whose care he was entrusted, proudly proclaimed himself his 'parent' and offered to meet his material needs within the limits of his income. He was upset by Dumo's reticence in requesting money from him. He cited a school trip to the Ciskei which Dumo did not mention out of consideration for the numerous calls on his uncle's limited resources.

The demands on Dumo's uncle's R1 100 monthly income were indeed considerable. He supported a household of thirteen people related in a complex manner defined as family. Dumo's uncle had a girlfriend who had her own child as well as a child born to their union. Dumo's maternal grand-aunt, Ouma Ncinci (literally little grandma), came at the invitation of her niece to stay with them in 1990 and acted as housekeeper – and parent – after Dumo's mother's departure to Paarl.

Ouma Ncinci was divorced from her own husband and had a boyfriend who had moved into this household as well, a factor which caused conflict with the head of the household, Dumo's uncle. There were two younger brothers to Dumo's uncle, one of whom had a child with a girlfriend whose family was given a share of groceries to feed the child. But it was the support of the three children of his unemployed sisters who lived in Khayelitsha that irked Dumo's uncle most. Dumo's uncle, however, philosophically accepted the onerous responsibilities which he felt fate had bestowed on him.

When I first met the thirteen-year-old Dumo early in the project, I was struck by his engaging personality. He was described by his family as gifted, respectful and reliable. He was doing well at school, was popular in his township soccer club and managed to stay out of trouble with the teachers by working hard. He was proud of his neat three-bedroom home, and was himself always neatly dressed.

Dumo understood the problems of children who ended up in gangs as stemming from inadequate educational provision and non-supportive adults, but he kept his distance from them. He set himself high goals in life – he wanted to be a lawyer to help the powerless in the wider society with a special focus on those in New Crossroads.

Despite Dumo's uncle's initial feelings about his responsibilities to his family, he came to believe he was being exploited by his kin. He had been carrying a heavy burden since his parents' death some twelve years earlier. He had been forced to abandon school with only Grade 10-level education and had started work as a labourer in a construction firm – a job he still had. He told me that he worked hard to ensure that he was not retrenched.

'It is very difficult for me to look after everyone,' he said. 'That is why I do not want to get married. No woman can take on the load of this family. I feel the pain. Even God will punish me for being too generous. My sisters just give birth and then leave their children with me without my knowing who their fathers are.'

It was hardly surprising that Dumo's uncle eventually threw in the towel. He left without a word to his family and went to live in Khayelitsha with his girlfriend and their children. The rest of the family was distressed, confused and somewhat bitter. They were particularly annoyed that he hadn't told them he was intending to leave.

Dumo took a philosophical view of this turn of events. He expressed the hope that his unemployed uncles would find work. His mother had to step in and support them from her base in Paarl out of her own meagre resources. Such support flies in the face of all the rules for married women who have to leave their families, including their own offspring, to devote themselves to their husbands' families.

Dumo's ability to bounce back after the many disappointments and discontinuities in the care he received was in part due to the firm foundations of the loving relationship he had with his mother. Their strong relationship enabled him to continue loving her in spite of her having 'abandoned' him. It was also a function of his mother's continued support from a distance. He visited her regularly and she came to visit him occasionally.

Dumo had personality traits that made it easy for him to attract and keep nurturing relationships. He was at ease with himself, well spoken, interested in his environment, and considerate. An attractive young man with an engaging smile playing perpetually around the corners of his mouth. His politeness did not get in the way of initiating conversations and asking searching questions. I was fascinated by him from the very beginning, and admired his facility for seeing the bright side of things.

III

The custom of separating children born before marriage from their mothers may have made sense in an era when the rate of births out of wedlock was low, and where such children could easily find loving care. But it's difficult explaining this practice when 70 per cent of all births are 'out of marriage'. Among the families of the sixteen adolescents who were part of the longer project, only six families entered marriage without children.

People in New Crossroads I spoke to felt that the practice continued because a child needed to 'belong' to the father's family. Without this sense of belonging the child would be adversely affected under the adoptive father's rituals. This view suggests that a male-dominated culture takes little account of the importance of mother-child relationships in cushioning the child against adversity.

Also, families were afraid that there would be conflict between the children who 'belong' and those deemed not to. Such conflicts arise in relation to seniority claims, particularly for male children who have a special standing within their families. They have ritual responsibilities in adulthood which give them standing so a child coming into a marriage with his mother poses a threat to the sons born to the new relationship.

I came across unhappiness among some of the adolescents in the project whose families had children born before marriage. Their uneasiness stemmed in part from the perceived threat to their status by a sibling born before the marriage of their parents. But a bigger problem seemed to have arisen in those cases where children born before marriage were not acknowledged by the parents. Should these children surface later, their siblings would feel cheated and lied to. How could they trust their parents, they asked? What other facts were being withheld?

Another fear was that should a child born before marriage come and live with the mother, its biological father would have an excuse to continue the relationship with the married woman resulting in marital conflict. I was quoted a Xhosa proverb which cautions against this danger: *Isiziba samanzi asihlali somile ukuba kwa kunetha imvula, amanzi aya ngqo kwesosiziba* – a spring does not stay dry forever. When the rain comes, water flows into it, it wells up again. The implication was that once two people have been lovers, there is always a chance that intimacy could occur again.

People felt that custom caused a lot of pain, but they felt bound by it. One woman in this bind was Pumla, which is not her real name. Her daughter was a disturbed teenage mother with no fixed place of abode.

PUMLA: Sometimes traditional rules bind us. Most men also think a child who is not his is the cause of the problems in marriage relationships because some children who go with their mothers to the new families still want to communicate with their real fathers. Like *isiko*, [customary practice], they want their own fathers' rituals. This can cause problems, as if the child wants to separate his mother and the stepfather.

Most of us do not know the danger we put our children into. Like the rumour I've heard that my daughter, Princess, says I do not love her. I chose a man who does not love her. I am concerned about her. I love her. That is why I am not happy with this man because I feel for her. If there was something I could do to make her understand that this man must rather go ... I do not sleep at night thinking about what she eats.

Rituals are very important so that your ancestors take care of you. For example, *imbeleko*. So if a child is born before marriage, you have already caused problems for that child.

Here was a woman torn between being bound by traditional customs and aware of the destructive impact the separation was having on her daughter. She wanted to leave her unhappy marriage and redeem her relationship with her estranged daughter.

Changing customs is difficult for communities and individuals where the customs are central, particularly when the greater society denies them human dignity, as happened during the apartheid years. Because there are few alternatives, people adhere to customs and beliefs and women and children bear the brunt of the trauma. It is unlikely that men, who see women and children as subjects of matrimonial negotiations between patrilineages, will initiate changes.

Women such as Pumla feel trapped by the need to identify with their ethnic culture and customs in spite of personal pain. She cannot conceive of herself as an autonomous being outside of this ethnic identity. The harsh world of male dominance and racism is too big for her to take on alone. She vacillates between her desire to nurture her daughter and obey Xhosa tradition and custom. Her responses to male dominance leave her unhappy and further diminish her self-esteem.

Women, clearly, have few options open to them. A male-headed household is still held as the romantic ideal in spite of the number of single female-headed households. When I asked the young people who they saw as their primary support all but one (she had been cared for by her sister) said it was mothers or grandmothers. This female-centred care-giving reflects an effective matrilineal community living alongside the myth of the male as the primary provider and leader of the household. It is this gap between ideal and reality that is confusing to the young people who are trying to make sense of their community and society in general. How are young people to understand their own evolving roles in a community that insists on male dominance even when men are absent physically or emotionally? How do young men learn how to become men in such a setting? What of young women who watch their strong mothers, grandmothers and sisters continue to subjugate themselves to men who are unable to meet their responsibilities as fathers, husbands and brothers? Yet increasingly women are insisting on playing more important roles within the marriage as co-providers.

It is also important to note that not all the experiences were necessarily traumatic. Lunga, for instance, felt he got the best out of those who raised him.

He was born in Old Crossroads in 1976. When I met him he was a tall seventeen-year-old with bright, alert eyes set in a broad face with a mischievous smile. Too many teeth were competing for space in his jaws, but he was unconcerned with this.

LUNGA: My mother told me that I was a few months old when she took me to my paternal grandmother and grandfather in Lady Frere in the Transkei. I then came back to live with my parents just before starting school. I started Grade 1 at Nomlinganiselo in 1985. I went out of school the very same year because I didn't have money. They wanted R5 for textbooks and I was forced to drop out.

The following year I went back to the Transkei and then I attended school full-time and I came to Cape Town for holidays. Later I stopped coming to Cape Town in December because my parents used to come to Lady Frere.

I shifted from the Transkei to the Ciskei, my mother's parents' home. I was still in Grade 3. When I arrived there I had a problem. They said since I came from the Transkei I did not know Afrikaans and in the Ciskei they start Afrikaans in Grade 1, so I was forced to stay in Grade 3 for another year. I was in class position three at the end of the year.

The next year I came back to Cape Town into Grade 4 in Khayelitsha. I came late to school and all the schools were full. I wanted to go to the Roman school [St Mary's] but they usually register their children the previous year in September or October. I was already late. So I went into Grade 4 Khayelitsha and then transferred to St Mary's until Grade 7.

At Lady Frere my granny from my father's side looked after me, and in the Ciskei it was my granny on my mother's side. For many years I was staying with my grannies. I only saw my parents in the holidays. So much so that I called my granny 'mother' and my mother, 'sisi' – sister.

The reason why I loved my grandmothers was because they were wonderful to me. The best part about being with my mother's mother was that my uncle was there and he looked after me very well. He bought me school uniforms and paid the school fees.

Clearly Lunga was well cared for by his grandparents despite the disruptions to his early schooling and the humiliation of being excluded from school for failing to pay the R5 fees. It is also clear that he has particularly fond memories of his uncle. (It turned out that the 'uncle' was actually his half-brother, born to his mother premaritally and left in the care of her parents. Lunga was only to learn of this much later.)

The difficulty of relating to his parents as parents is symbolised by his referring to his mother as sisi. She was indeed his sister, given that she had ceded her parental responsibilities to her parents, an admission that she herself was still a child who needed to be assisted. Nor had they overcome the tensions of their sibling/mother/child relationship. She regarded the matter as closed whereas he felt there was much still to be discussed, although he had no way of telling her this.

I asked him about his feeling when he first came to Cape Town. About how it felt being reunited with his parents. About how often he managed to see his grandparents.

LUNGA: When I first came to live here I was afraid to ask anything from my parents, even money. I had problems. I was so used to my father's mother that even when my parents were there [at his granny's home] for the holidays I couldn't go to my parents and ask them for anything. I would go to my granny and ask her.

I was about ten years old when I started to live with my mother and father on a full-time basis again. My granny from Lady Frere is afraid to come this side [to Cape Town]. She only came once into town. We sometimes go and visit them with my parents.

It was not only the physical distance between Lunga and his parents which led to problems in re-establishing their relationship. There was also evidence of a big psychological gulf between them. This was in part due to the different parenting styles between his parents and grandparents. He saw his grandparents as having been more affirming of him, whereas he felt his parents did not show him respect or listen to him.

I asked him who he turned to when he had a problem? His response was prompt and emphatic.

LUNGA: I speak with my friends, not with my parents. They are cruel, the parents. That is why we mustn't bring things to them. For example, one day my friend was sent on an errand and lost R10. His family pestered him about it. It was said that I was also with him so I was beaten. But I wasn't with him when he lost the money. They said that I should pay for it. I didn't pay for it. They didn't follow it up. It ended there. But I was angry. If a child has done something wrong parents tend not to discuss the problem and show him what is right or what is wrong. They just beat and beat and beat and beat and beat and beat. Parents end up giving up. They then let the child do what he wants to do.

Parents should listen to the problems of their children. If a child has a problem parents should speak to the child. There are only a few parents who do that – too few of them. Children should also study because being educated is a great benefit. If you don't study you will never find work because there are many people who are unemployed. I wish to finish school and come to the University of Cape Town.

Lunga's case raises an issue of discipline. He told me his grannies never beat him, 'only pinched' him if he had misbehaved.

In the New Crossroads community children are disciplined from a young age through encouragement and shaming, corporal punishment and, increasingly, by demands on children to perform domestic chores.

Shaming is a major tactic. As the child ages shaming is coupled to physical punishment which, in extreme cases, can turn sadistic. In New Crossroads shaming was seen as drawing attention to an individual's weaknesses or vulnerability: *umntu ungumntu ngabanye abantu* – a person is a person through the connectedness to others. It also fostered interdependence in the community by openly recognising the individual's weaknesses, and yet still accepting them.

Families who used shaming argued that by drawing attention to the child's inadequacy or disability within a caring family relationship, the child would be less vulnerable to the vicious teasing they might face in the hostile outside world. However, shaming also meant that high performers are referred to disparagingly as 'bookworms' with a mixture of envy and pride in their extraordinary talents.

On many occasions during the project I was made aware of the lasting impact shaming seems to have on vulnerable adolescents. As victims of shaming at home, at school and in the wider community, they, in turn, use shaming and mockery with devastating effect on their peers. Shaming and mocking laughter were at the centre of many of the disputes I had to mediate during our weekends away. For example, I had earlier identified one of the youngsters as having visual problems. He was helped acquire a pair of glasses.

This intervention was instructive. The teenager's school had not detected his visual problems which we noticed immediately. The day hospital that was to get him free glasses would not see him after school. In the end a fieldworker had to accompany him through the bureaucratic maze. Then he faced being mocked mercilessly as Number-Four-Eyes [Four-eyed person].

The depth of the wounds inflicted on the ego by shaming showed up time and again in some sensitive adolescents. Take Xola. At the age of fourteen he told me that he was still struggling to come to terms with some of the things that had been said to, and about, him.

XOLA: The older boys and other older people used to laugh at me when I was beaten by my mother. They said that I was not her son but a child of baboons which was why she beat me so much. I ended up wondering if they were right. I was worried about that for a long time.

There was little realisation of the impact on his self-confidence and self-esteem by those who mocked him, let alone empathy from his mother who not only beat him, but did not stop the mockery.

Corporal punishment in New Crossroads had widespread use among both parents and teachers. In some cases I found the children had come to expect and accept it. Of course the severity varied widely: some of the children had never been beaten at home, others received regular beatings for trivial reasons. Lunga has already mentioned that his parents beat him because they were cruel. Another youngster, Mthetheleli Kwakwa, was beaten so badly he had scars.

Mthetheleli was ten years old when he joined the project. One day he told me he had been severely beaten by his father at the behest of his mother. It was not the first time this had happened. He also showed me scars on his back from a beating he had received a year before. Mthetheleli had a scarred face – testimony to other assaults. He could not make eye contact with anybody. He was fidgety and lacked self-confidence. His clothing was dirty. He was a child crying out for love and care. On one of our first weekend trips with him he burst into tears when we arrived at the beach cottage in Cape Point. When I asked him what was the matter he said that he was so hungry that he could not wait for supper.

I interviewed both Mthetheleli's parents and his paternal grandmother at their extraordinarily filthy home, where the marks of poverty and degradation were everywhere in evidence: the pungent smell of urine, soiled nappies stacked high in the bathroom, the infant running around without much clothing on in mid-winter.

Both Mthetheleli's parents were employed, their combined monthly income being R1 000 in 1991. His mother came home late every day from her job as a cleaner. Neither of the parents ever did household chores. The burden of cleaning, childcare and laundry fell on Mthetheleli and his ten-year-old cousin. There was an uncle, a relative of his father's, who took care of the family wealth in the form of nine goats and was paid R50 weekly for doing so by Mthetheleli's father. Mthetheleli was, however, also expected to help with herding these goats because his father insisted that he develop the skills to survive in the rural areas. He hoped that his family would eventually settle there once he had made enough money to run his own business.

MR KWAKWA: I first came to Cape Town in 1970 and my wife came to visit me in 1973. We were married in 1968 and we lived in the Transkei where we were both born. While I was working in Cape Town my wife lived with my mother. All of the children were born there, except the last born who was born in Cape Town in 1990.

The family has always had money problems and that is why I decided to bring my wife to Cape Town so that she could also lessen the financial burdens by working. I started working as a 'boy' in the Welkom mines. The conditions there were very bad. Before going underground each miner was given an injection, here in the chest with a long needle like a cattle needle. These injections made us lose our fear.

We did very strenuous exercises in a very small space. You had to crawl on your hands and knees. We wore pads on our knees like the cricket players. As we crawled through the small passages it was as if water was running in furrows on either side of us but it was streams of our own sweat. When I first started working on the mines we earned R11 a month. At that time it was difficult to get a job if you were not born in the city so I took a contract with the mines.

After a year in the mines I decided to come to Cape Town. This was in 1970. I was living in Langa Hostel. Conditions in the hostels were also bad because you would find three beds in a very small room, each bed being the 'home' of the migrant worker. I moved out of the bedroom and lived in a small pantry where people kept their groceries and I made it my room. My wife only visited when we wanted another child.

Mr Kwakwa understood the source of his impoverishment. He had experienced being excluded from jobs as a rural African and this had affected his family fortunes. The pain of being treated as a 'boy' was still acute. It was little wonder that to salvage his manhood he demanded absolute obedience from his family.

MRS KWAKWA: Even though we were struggling financially we did not think of family planning. When I visited Cape Town I had a bad time because I had to hide from the inspectors and the *amabhulu*, the boers, since I had no rights to stay in the city. One day I was caught by the boers while visiting my husband at his work in Milnerton. He worked on a farm. I was without a reference book. I was eight months pregnant. That was in 1973. I slept for two nights in Pollsmoor prison because my husband did not have money when I was arrested. Truly I experienced bad things while visiting Cape Town.

When I came to Cape Town my mother-in-law looked after the children in the Transkei. She also helped financially. She had goats and cows and also a garden with green vegetables. There was a very bad time of drought when we suffered because many goats died and the garden was dry and dead. That is also one of the reasons why I decided to come to Cape Town to join my husband permanently in 1978. We lived in a shack in Old Crossroads since the pantry in Langa hostel was too small. I had arrived in Cape Town with two children.

In Old Crossroads we had a bad time because it was the time when the residents of Crossroads were fighting with the township people. On the other side the boers were giving us a tough time because they removed us from Old Crossroads. Raising children there was very difficult. I remember one day my neighbour's children were burnt to death because of the fighting. I decided not to have my children with me. I took them all back to live with their granny in the Transkei, *emaXhoseni*.

I had a baby boy in 1980 called Mthetheleli and I also took him to the Transkei to his granny. I never had a chance of staying with my children full-time because I was sometimes in Cape Town and sometimes in the Transkei. I tried to discipline my children but I had no say because the person they trusted was their granny. They trust her more than me.

When it comes to discipline it is very hard because each one of us has a different way of disciplining. The granny is old and cannot discipline. Instead she is spoiling the children.

My family is a very strong one which has survived hardships of poverty and the bad laws of this country. I remember a day when I was caught for the reference book while pregnant. The baby was born very healthy in spite of the bad conditions in Pollsmoor prison where I slept.

Mthetheleli is a normal child. Sometimes he is naughty because the other day he was severely punished by his father. He likes his father's goats – sometimes he sleeps with them in the backyard when it is warm. Sometimes he does sleep out because the house is locked and I am working shifts and I am not home most of the time. I work from five in the morning to eleven at night. The other shift comes in at twelve at night. Sometimes when there has been violence we are asked to sleep over at the workplace.

I love Mthetheleli and he loves me. I find my role as a mother confusing and difficult. My husband and the granny are always undermining my authority over the children.

MR KWAKWA: I want to discipline my children stringently so that they know how to look after themselves. I find this difficult since my mother is the one staying with the children.

I want my children to know about farming, about ploughing, looking after animals. What I really want to do is to go back to the Transkei and to open a business one day. Life is difficult here. I earn little money but I have managed to maintain my family. Did you see that car out there? I just need to fix it and we can drive back to the Transkei.

Disciplining the children is very hard because they spend little time with us. Even if we try to be strict it does not help because they will go back to the Transkei and they will repeat the same mistakes. Well, it is difficult to say because we can't really have them here in Cape Town all the time.

When it comes to Mthetheleli, he is a naughty child. I gave him two strong warnings because of what he had been doing and then the third time I beat him. First of all, my sixth child was nearly knocked down by a car when Mthetheleli was looking after her. Then Mthetheleli climbed up on the roof with his little sister and held her by her legs with her head hanging down. The third time this little girl told us that Mthetheleli had put her in a sewerage manhole which was empty and had closed the lid. He nearly suffocated the child. That day I beat him severely. He even had bruises on his back.

But basically Mthetheleli is a promising child. He even shows an interest in the goats which we have here. Mthetheleli wants a person to keep an eye on him because he is a very naughty child. If you do not watch him, something terrible will happen. After the first trail [a reference to the wilderness weekends] I noticed that his violence had decreased a little although he is still like that, and his watching videos has also decreased. Because he is bored most of the time, he thinks of doing mischief.

Mthetheleli's grandmother also had opinions about the different styles of discipline. While we talked in the sitting room the Kwakwa's youngest child was strapped to her back and two other little children played in the kitchen and passage. The one child was a little girl, the Kwakwa's child, the other was a very handsome little boy who was the child of the Kwakwa's eldest daughter who had run away from home. I was told that the eldest granddaughter vanished without trace into the sands of the Cape Flats.

It was a cold day and the little boy in the kitchen had on a small jacket with nothing beneath it and the little girl a short cotton dress. Grandmother Kwakwa was seventy-eight years old. She had a very loving relationship with the little boy on her back who gazed at me and who, when he was unwound from the blanket, kept very close to her touching her and kissing her. I noticed that there was neither food in the house nor any sign of cooking. When asked about Mthetheleli, Grandmother Kwakwa described him as very naughty.

'Both parents are very strict and harsh with the children,' she said. 'Mthetheleli goes out with big boys, his cousins, to watch videos in the neighbourhood. One Saturday Mthetheleli took three cigarettes from the cousin while the cousin was drunk and when I asked him what he was doing he said he was keeping them for the next day because usually when the cousin is drunk he smokes the whole box.'

While Mr Kwakwa dealt with his powerlessness by resorting to fantasies – his hoped-for business, his car (a hopeless wreck), a life in the rural areas – and imposed his authority on his family, Mrs Kwakwa slipped into depression. As she got to trust me she admitted to physical and sexual abuse within her marriage. But her attitude towards her husband and her son, Mthetheleli, remained ambivalent.

One day a fieldworker happened to call in at the house while Mthetheleli was being beaten. His father was hitting him with a sjambok on the face for having lost fifteen cents while on an errand for his mother. Mrs Kwakwa admitted to instigating the beating to discipline Mthetheleli. It was only through the intervention of the fieldworker that the beating stopped. A day later Mthetheleli was still in severe pain, with a swollen eye and bruises all over his face. The only comforter was the drunken uncle who used ice begged from neighbours to cool off the throbbing and to stop the bleeding.

Some days later Mrs Kwakwa was remorseful and tried to make up to her son by buying him new clothing.

At other times the fieldworker found her sitting dejected, surrounded by filth. Ironically she worked at a childcare centre taking care of other people's children. Worn down by these long hours and her emotional burdens, she was too drained to nurture her own children.

At the time I feared for Mthetheleli's future. Our last meeting was in 1998. He'd grown into a strong young man, but the vulnerability and insecurity remained. He lacked the most basic social graces.

Given the widespread use of corporal punishment, the children of New Crossroads have come to accept it as part of their interaction with adults. In their conversations with me they often referred to corporal punishment in a matter-of-fact way.

On one of the wilderness weekends I had a particularly rowdy group of youngsters who could not contain their excitement about being away from home, and the novelty of sleeping in a group at a beach cottage. They jumped up and down on the beds, they had pillow fights, they ran in and out of the cottage, agitated by a bright full moon. The trail leader and I repeatedly tried to calm them down, but failed. We had to abandon any hope of sleep that night.

The next morning I talked sternly to them and made them promise to behave. At the end of the weekend they noted in their trail reports how remarkable it was that we did not beat them because they felt that they deserved nothing less.

It is this acceptance of corporal punishment that is likely to perpetuate its use when they are themselves parents. In fact most of the youngsters regularly beaten at home said they would beat their children as a last resort, or if the children were to disgrace them in any way. Asked to define the 'disgrace' referred to, they said if the child was to put them to shame.

A combination of a strong shaming custom and an authoritarian-autocratic parenting style might well be perpetuated by the next generation.

Unexpectedly a community meeting arranged to give the residents of New Crossroads feedback on the project provided further insights into this issue. I reported the concern children expressed about being beaten on a regular basis both at home and at school. I also voiced concern about the random beating of children that I'd witnessed at a previous community meeting. On that occasion a few adults, including the chairman of the Civic Association, whipped the children to drive them out of the pre-school building which was too small to accommodate both parents and children for the meeting.

After a few minutes' discussion it was suggested that we should talk about more important things. Most parents felt that there was no alternative to corporal punishment, and that it was a non-issue.

V

Most of the adolescents I worked with complained about being overburdened with domestic chores from a young age. They had to help get the family ready for work or school in the mornings by getting up early to cook breakfast (usually porridge) and make beverages for the adults. After-school responsibilities included cleaning the home, taking care of siblings, and preparing the evening meal.

There was no overt gender discrimination in the allocation of domestic chores, although some boys managed to get out of duties by feigning incompetence. Some of the girls claimed to prefer sole responsibility for domestic chores in return for presents of fashionable clothes and other luxuries. The long-term implications of such trade-offs for the girls are considerable. On the one hand learning to play the traditional role of domestic worker and care provider may serve a useful purpose in a traditional society; on the other hand the increasing demands on women to be self-sufficient would render a 'conditioned' young woman unequal to the task.

Gender discrimination in domestic responsibilities intensifies around the age of eighteen after boys have been initiated into manhood. Real men are not supposed to do 'women's work'. There are major tensions evident in New Crossroads and in society in general that women feel emboldened by the country's new constitution which entrenches gender equality. The constitution's precepts, however, have yet to find expression in the lives of New Crossroads residents.

My sense is that most children in New Crossroads carry an enormous load of household responsibilities. I remember Phalo's anger when he talked about being made to run errands which sometimes involved long walks in the rain or heat. Mthetheleli had also told me that he became abusive to his younger sister when the strain of looking after her overcame him. What with his domestic chores and waking up at five to herd his father's goats he would often fall asleep in class. This never bothered his parents.

If there was little communication and trust between the generations then there was also an abrupt ending of tenderness between parent and child after the toddler stage. Compounding this is the conflict-ridden relationships between parents and adolescents. There is little scope for teenage experimentation and because the environment is unsafe, parents feel that they cannot take the risk of giving their children any leeway.

In this regard Phalo was a case in point. He was one of the most troubled adolescents in the project and ended up in a reformatory after repeated petty crimes. Phalo was the most charming, handsome young man in the group and wore his worn-out clothes that were too small for him with a measure of dignity. He never freely participated in any discussion, responding only to direct questions and never elaborately. My attempts at drawing him into the circle failed. He remained aloof but friendly. The only time I encountered him in a relaxed mode was at a stop street in the Claremont shopping area where he was begging for money with his friends. He flashed his charming smile as he recognised me and came to ask me for money. I had to fight against my natural instincts and turned him down knowing that the money was not to be used for purposes of which I would approve.

PHALO'S MOTHER, MRS NKUHLU: Phalo was born in Old Crossroads in 1976. He is our eighth child: two boys and six girls. As a child he was very sweet and when he started school in 1983 he was still fine. Something bad happened [in 1992] when he no longer wanted to go to school. When I asked him the reason he said that the teachers were beating him. I explained to him the danger of not going to school because his older brothers and sisters are suffering now. With them we did not have money to send them to school.

My husband worked at a municipality in Nyanga as a plumber. I was never formally employed. Something strange happened in 1984 when Phalo was in Grade 2. His father was fired from work for no reason. According to the employer my husband was aggressive so they could no longer keep him. We knew it was witchcraft and we did not bother begging them to take him back. He then learnt carpentry and does odd jobs for people in the township. I also help with a bit of sewing so that we can maintain the family. It is difficult sometimes because there is little food inside the house.

I think this witchcraft is here in New Crossroads because Phalo is smoking dagga. He sometimes begs in the streets for money not to buy food, but to buy dagga. His friends make him smoke and sometimes I suspect drugs because his eyes are red.

Phalo does not want to go to school anymore. He involves himself with boys who do not go to school. I am worried because he does not even take the *ixhwele's* [herbalist's] medicine which would help him with this problem. Sometimes he does not sleep at home. He is close to his father who also loves him.

I tried to get your address because after his first outing he was behaving very well and talked about the care which they had received [on the wilderness weekends]. Unfortunately I could not phone because I wanted your advice about reformatories. He is hardly at home and always in need of money.

He has been arrested three times and at the moment he is waiting for the trial. The other two charges were dropped because of his age. The last case was when he stole bicycles in Claremont. The other day he robbed a shop in Claremont. I do not know the details because you cannot get the truth from him.

The other children behave very well. I cannot talk about the child who has isolated himself, *uphuma ecaleni* [the strayed one]. Otherwise they listen to me.

Mrs Nkuhlu also supports corporal punishment in the schools. When I asked her about the quality of the schools she said: 'They are fine. The only problem is that these children complain about beating, and I told them beating is the best thing. We were beaten also but we did not complain. If a child is late for school that child must be beaten so that they do not come late tomorrow.'

She remained unwavering in spite of being reminded of a Xhosa proverb which cautioned about too much use of the rod: *Induku ay-inamzi* – the rod has no home, or beating destroys homes.

'Yes, it's true but we have to use it, we have to beat,' she insisted.

Asked about her views of talking to a child and letting him express feelings, and showing him his mistakes and encouraging him not to repeat them, she said: 'Yes, we do that. You show the child that this is not the right thing. Then you beat because the child will go outside and will get the wrong kind of teachers in the streets and then you will see your child start drinking and doing all the bad things. It's a pity with Phalo because *andisena ngalo* – I don't have a strong arm any more. I would beat him if I did.'

Phalo's mother believed children should listen and not speak. Phalo felt he was used by his parents and sisters to run errands. No one seemed to feel sorry for him or treat him with respect. Phalo also talked about being hungry. 'If there is no food we just sit or we watch TV.' Then he told me why he'd dropped out of school.

PHALO: It [the school] was nice but the only problem was that I just sat down and didn't want to go to the school anymore. We were beaten and they made us pick up papers. It was always my wish to go to school but now I don't want to. I told my mother that I am not interested in going to that school.

The reason that I dropped out of Zolani School was that my mother always said that I had not come from school although I had come from school. That bothered me so – *yandikhathaza*. I told her to ask my friends and she never asked them. I told her to go to school and to ask. She never went. I was very angry and I decided to stop going to school. I hated this thing of my mother saying that I was not from school whereas I was from school.

Parents do not sit with us around the table and let us express our ideas. When I need to talk about something, I sometimes go to my father.

Phalo felt that his mother mistrusted him, and that undermined his confidence in tackling the outside world, including school. He felt totally abandoned. It was hardly surprising that Phalo could not recall an occasion on which he felt really free and happy. 'Not with me. I have never experienced that situation,' he said.

And what about his dreams of the future?

'I want to be a traffic cop and to catch people in the streets!' He laughed. Probably at himself.

With such little support from his family or school Phalo took risks to spite his mother and to distance himself from the pain their relationship caused him. His fantasy about becoming a traffic policeman 'to catch people' was an apparent outlet for his anger against a society that had failed him.

This failure led to his tragic death midway through the project. He went off with his friends and later his body was found in a street not far from his home. He had multiple gunshot wounds. He had been killed execution-style.

VI

In spite of the professed adherence to an incest taboo, child abuse including sexual violence against children, has reached epidemic proportions in South Africa. The statistics continue to rise but these figures are merely the tip of an iceberg. Many more cases go unreported, and the silence that protects family honour contributes to under-reporting. The rape figures too are more than alarming. The justice system is ineffective and lack of proper training has left many policemen bewildered. Parents feel unprotected and unable to protect their own offspring from the brutality of a violent society. Young men who are brutalised by the legacy of apartheid are themselves brutalising others. Women are targeted by angry, frustrated men. With this goes an ever-increasing rate of HIV/Aids. The commonly held myth that sex with a virgin by an infected person leads to cleansing is lethal. Everyday countless innocent young girls are sentenced to death by those holding this belief. The country is sitting on a time bomb.

New Crossroads is no exception in this regard. Many children suffer sexual assaults in silence. Usually mothers are part of the silence.

I was told by many members of the project that they knew someone in their neighbourhood who was abused by a relative or friend of the family. Indeed I heard of a girl who ran away from home when she was abused by her mother's husband's brother. She had been born before the marriage. Despite her complaints her mother's husband refused to act. The mother later regretted her failure to protect her daughter. Will the daughter ever understand the dynamics? I fear there are many similar cases.

CHAPTER FIVE

School

Verwoerd's ghost

I

The African National Congress's 1955 Freedom Charter promised that 'the doors of learning shall be open'. This commitment formed the core of the liberation package directed at securing the future. The authors of this laudable sentiment had however not fully appreciated the constraining impact of Bantu Education on the capacity of the majority of Africans to utilise the open 'doors of learning' after years of having been shut out. Indeed it is doubtful that Dr H F Verwoerd, the architect of Bantu Education and the intellectual force behind the enforcement of apartheid, knew how profound an impact he would have on the future. In making the statement that 'the Bantu child must not be made to aspire to green pastures where he shall never be allowed to graze', he erected a wall between young black people and their future success. Verwoerd's ghost continues to haunt the schools of post-apartheid South Africa, as Nana, one of the girls in the project I was particularly struck by, made clear.

She was a self-confident, attractive teenager, and the only one out of the sixteen fortunate enough to have always lived with both parents.

NANA: I lived with my parents in Old Crossroads in a shack. When the shacks in Old Crossroads were burnt down, people moved to New Crossroads. That is where I was brought up. I later attended school from Grade 1 to 7 at Nomlinganiselo Primary School.

The school was built in 1981 and opened its doors in 1982. The school has enjoyed stable leadership since its inception. More teachers were employed between 1987 and 1989, while others left. Those who have left are Nomkolite who teaches at Khayelitsha now and Miss Maphisa who is now in Johannesburg. She got married recently. Many students have also left the school to study in 'coloured' schools or other 'black' schools.

The school has its ups and downs. Some days are happy and others are difficult. There are too many unnecessary deaths from living in a dangerous area. For example, one of my classmates died in a car accident. Another pupil was injured going home from school.

People in New Crossroads have different approaches to life. Children are unruly and apt to retaliate if disciplined by adults. At school teachers whip children a lot. Teachers try their best to help children to work harder, but it is all confusing. Our school in New Crossroads seems to be quite good because pupils get to pass to higher grades.

But there is another thing. Some teachers are not so clear when they teach. They just give us tests to write and when we fail they lash us. They do not seem to realise that we do not understand what they have taught us. They do not give us a chance to ask questions. There is a particularly cruel teacher in our school. She hits us on our hands and fingers, sometimes thirty-eight lashes. Some teachers lash us on the body. Those teachers really punish us in a way we are not supposed to be punished. This is extreme punishment.

Most children in New Crossroads have lost respect for older people. They see adults as cruel. Some have become quite obstinate, rude and they swear at older people. Even those with disabilities and senior citizens are treated with disrespect. Unnecessary punishment tends to trigger this reaction because when children complain, they are threatened with even greater and more severe punishment.

Many children do not attend school anymore because of fear of being lashed severely when they make a mistake. If a child comes to the school with a parent after having been beaten, the teacher tells the parent to leave the child in his or her training if the parent wants the child to learn. The child gets beaten again by the teacher because the parent complained.

School trips are also a source of disagreements between parents and teachers. For example, on one occasion a trip for the students was suggested at a parents' meeting. One of our teachers walked out of the room because she wanted to be in charge of everything. The trip was to cost R300 but it was postponed to the following year instead of happening at the end of the last term. On many such trips money often disappears without trace.

At a farewell for the Grade 7s an award for neatness, diligence, and academic performance is given. It is a great occasion that serves to motivate pupils to work hard. Our teachers try their best but they are wrong to lash us so severely.

At school I meet many children where we mix and share ideas. Our school is the first to have a farewell party for the Grade 7s. We also celebrate International Children's Day and Environment Day. Today we went to the Waterfront to meet and mingle with children from different ethnic groups. It was not the first time that I had gone to the Waterfront but it was so for many other children. We enjoyed what we saw at the Waterfront. Our teacher told us that he used to go to the Waterfront when he lived in Mowbray. He is originally from the Transvaal and he began teaching in 1978 in Bloemfontein and he has visited Swaziland. This teacher's parents are well educated. His father was at UCT and his mother studied in Richard's Bay. Some of the children he taught are now grown up. He emphasised the importance of education and its purpose in society. He is a good teacher but some teachers cannot teach properly because they don't have the heart to teach children. They become furious when asked questions.

Nana's story brings out many of the complexities of township education: the coexistence of good and bad teachers; attempts by teachers and parents to enrich the learning environments of their children; problems of corporal punishment etc. Good teachers are depicted as those with 'a heart to teach children' and the confidence to answer questions as well as to expose children to a wider world. The teacher Nana singled out for special praise is an example of the advantage of being brought up in a well-to-do family with educated parents. The teacher's self-confidence and competence can be linked to his good home environment and the love for education instilled in him early in life.

In contrast, poor performing teachers lack self-confidence, tend to be threatened by questions from pupils, to use corporal punishment, and to bully both pupils and their parents. The female teacher Nana referred to seems to be a particularly difficult person. Her insistence on control of money matters also raises the sceptre of misuse of funds collected for school trips and other communal purposes. I was told of numerous instances of funds disappearing without trace. Such occurrences breed mistrust between and amongst parents, pupils, and teachers.

Nonetheless, Nomlinganiselo is the better of the two government primary schools serving New Crossroads. The other, Andile Primary School, is said to experience greater difficulties. The headmaster of Nomlinganiselo Primary School has linked up with the University of Cape Town's School of Education to improve teachers' competence. The problem of children with learning difficulties, which tends to be ignored by the entire education system for African children, is a special focus of this partnership. In the larger group in my project, three adolescents had major learning problems and could neither read nor write although they were in Grade 5 and above.

St Mary's is a Roman Catholic primary school which also serves New Crossroads. It stands head and shoulders above the other two. It is the school of choice for those parents in New Crossroads and surrounding townships with professional jobs or who have high goals for their children. Its team of eleven teachers is headed by a woman who is herself a product of the school and determined to keep it successful. The philosophy of the school is to work in partnership with parents to instil pride and responsibility in pupils for high achievement. Parents are obliged to participate in school meetings and programmes as part of a social contract between the school and the community.

'Apha eRoma [here at the Roman Catholic school] there are some qualities which you won't find at other schools,' I was told by the head teacher. 'We have certain values which I think do not exist at other schools. One of them is that we take a personal interest in our children. For instance, if a child is sick we do not phone the parents and tell them to come and fetch their child. We take the child to the clinic and later report to the parents that this or that happened. We also follow up on all problem cases. Our parents are free to come and complain or to query anything so that we can discuss things together with them.'

St Mary's method of discipline also contrasts sharply with what Nana describes above. Discipline is based on positive reinforcement. Punishment is rarely meted out. Non-corporal disciplinary means are used: no play time, cleaning the school premises and other chores. The teaching style is engaging. The teachers use drama and a hands-on introduction of new themes which encourages participation by the pupils. They have a music group which teaches pupils to play marimba drums. African and classical European music genres are celebrated and taught with equal enthusiasm. Some graduates of the school have gone on to become performers and have influenced other pupils in the high schools they attended.

When I visited the school the staff complement was female except for the mathematics and science teacher, who was a coloured man. The school vibrated with enthusiasm. The team spirit among the teachers was infectious. The staff room was neat and decorated with pictures of contemporary South African leaders who had visited the school, such as Chris Hani who had visited the school a few weeks before his assassination. There were other beautiful decorations adorning the walls and cupboards. A well-kept garden and playground enhanced the school environment.

The teachers showed me their improvised library – each classroom had a neatly stacked box of books from READ, a non-governmental organisation that promotes reading in all schools in disadvantaged areas. I noticed that some of the books dealt with themes from the contemporary New Crossroads environment. These themes were the product of some teachers in the group who contributed material towards the books. For example, 'the family' was depicted as grandmother, mother and a little boy – a departure from the idealised nuclear family of father and mother with son and daughter. Some of the stories were about lost goats – a common feature of this township. Pupils enjoyed reading about real-life issues and seeing their own experiences captured in the written word.

The teachers attributed the good results the school attained to their positive attitude, the commitment of parents, and the role of the pre-school in preparing children for learning. Grade 1 teachers talked about the striking differences between 'granny children' and those with pre-school exposure. 'Granny children' were slow to adjust, and tended to stay home in the wet Cape winters.

Gender differences also drew comment from the perceptive teachers. They said that girls tended to be much brighter than boys at primary school; they were consistent workers, did their homework and got good grades at all levels. Boys were said to be more playful and distracted. For the majority of boys the focus was on peer-group relations from which they derived satisfaction and affirmation of their self-esteem. Teachers attributed the drop in the standard of performance by girls in high school to the shift in focus amongst adolescent girls towards sexual liaisons with boys. At this stage girls became increasingly preoccupied with their looks and acceptability to others. Affirmation and self-esteem were increasingly sought from peer-group members. Academic performance suffered as a result.

St Mary's School also faced the problem of not being subsidised by the government because of a principled stand by the Catholic Church. The church refused to register the school under the apartheid system. This laudable protest denied them access to certain state resources. In particular, teachers felt that they could have benefited from free textbooks and other school equipment now in short supply. They also felt left out of the government housing subsidy scheme available to teachers in government schools. Nonetheless, on balance they recognised that they had a better working environment.

II

I also visited the only high school in New Crossroads, Stembele Matiso. It is a caricature of what an educational institution ought to be. On one of my early visits to the school, after repeated attempts to see the headmaster, I arrived to learn that he was again not available despite pre-confirmed arrangements to see him and his staff. I was told he had been forced by militant teachers, as was the case with other headmasters from the African townships, to go to the Provincial Department of Education in Cape Town to convey teachers demands for refunds of deducted pay for previous teacher stay-aways from work. Teachers and pupils were idly standing around the premises. One of many days when there was no teaching.

The school building was relatively new and reasonably well equipped, but it looked run down. A pile of broken desks had been dumped in the open space between classrooms adding to the untidy appearance of the place. These desks must have been in this position for a while given that weeds were growing between the wreckage.

What was left of the lawn was overgrown. Garbage, especially loose paper, was flying in the southeaster drawing no visible response from the apathetic teachers and pupils listlessly milling around. The headmaster's office was dusty and uninviting. The only bright object in the office was a beautiful photograph of the headmaster's daughter in a traditional Venda outfit. The deputy headmaster claimed to have had no idea about my visit. Our numerous letters to the school and a copy of our annual research report had not succeeded in awakening an interest in the work the project was doing with young people in the township.

My meeting with the teachers confirmed my worst fears. They were a demoralised group of people. Many of the women teachers were grossly overweight. Some of the men had visible signs of heavy alcohol abuse. None of them could clearly express themselves in English in spite of the requirement that they should teach all content subjects in English. How they managed to communicate with pupils, let alone add value to the learning process, is a mystery.

The atmosphere was tense. There was an air of impending doom. The teachers were shifting around in their seats and not focussing on what we had to say. An anxious woman teacher came up to me and whispered in my ear. She urged me and my colleagues to drive off immediately. She feared what would happen to us once the protest march, which was about to start, got under way. The presence of Patti Henderson, a white woman on the research team, was seen as highly provocative. It was feared that some of the young people could see her as a target for their anger against white racism. Her fears were based on reality – the brutal murder of Amy Biehl, a young American white woman who was killed some months earlier in a tragic mob attack in Guguletu by angry young people. I decided the best option was to leave.

III

Relationships between teachers and pupils at high-school level are also complicated by the rebelliousness of adolescents. The age-old struggle to define an identity, experimentation with drugs, alcohol and cigarettes all complicate relationships with adults. The presence of teachers who are themselves alcohol abusers worsens matters.

Tuleka, one of the adolescents from the group of sixteen, was a pupil at Stembele Matiso. She had many sad stories to tell about this school. One incident occurred when a schoolgirl, who had been drinking with some teachers in a nearby shebeen, became unruly. She threatened those trying to restrain her and vowed 'to beat the shit out of anyone' who dared to touch her.

I was unable to obtain official records of matric results from Stembele Matiso from the Department of Education in the Western Province as the department had an agreement with the teachers' trade union not to release results of individual schools to the public. However, from informal evidence, it was clear that this school had one of the worst records of matriculation results. Interviews with the young people on the project and their parents indicated that few pupils ever passed matric in this school, and none ever wrote science or mathematics on the higher-grade level.

Increasingly parents living in New Crossroads were giving up on the township school system and sending their children to schools outside the township. They clearly felt unable to do anything about the nearby schools and saw the opening up of schools as an opportunity. The poorest sent their children back to rural areas in the Eastern Cape Province in the hope that there would be more order in rural settings as was traditionally the case.

The next best option was sending your child to nearby former coloured schools. Under the apartheid dispensation these schools had better resources, and better matric performance records. Their proximity to African townships with lower commuting costs was an attractive consideration. The disadvantage for many residents of New Crossroads was the use of Afrikaans in coloured schools as many African township schools did not offer Afrikaans on the higher grade. A few coloured schools also used Afrikaans as a medium of instruction – a serious barrier for most African pupils.

The best option, however, was access to former white schools. This was an opportunity open to only the relatively well off, mainly the children of professionals. A small but significant number got financial assistance from their parents' employers which enabled them to enrol in these privileged schools. (Ironically, the drive towards greater equity in resource allocation to schools has led to large increases in fees, making these previously racially segregated schools more and more unaffordable for the poor people.)

IV

A common thread running through the stories of the sixteen teenagers in the project was the frequency with which they changed schools. A major reason was a search for better opportunities. In some cases changes were rapid and highly disruptive. What amazed me was how children and parents were able to put up with this chopping and changing. Such was their desperation that they were on a constant search for better alternatives.

Changes in the family life also impacted on the pupils. Dumo, who was the most promising among the young men at the age of fourteen, ended up dropping out of school when his mother remarried and left him. The further abandonment of the family by his mother's brother left the children exposed to the worst problems of poverty and vulnerability. Dumo ended up as an unskilled labourer in a factory, facing a future of low wages and job insecurity.

During their high school career only four of the sixteen escaped changing schools – this stability partly explains Bulelani's success. Many of the pupils repeated grades and all those in the project were above the age norm for their grades. Even the two most successful ones were nineteen and twenty years old when they graduated from high school.

Bulelani's story shows the extent to which parents would go to provide better educational opportunities for their children. His mother's determination to overcome barriers knew no bounds. To approach the Rhodes High School headmaster must have taken enormous courage and desperation.

But the ones who escape the township school system face other risks. Those left behind because their parents had neither the material nor moral resources to carve a path for them turn their rage against those seen to have 'sold out'. The rage at feeling left out expresses itself in a variety of ways, taunts of 'playing white' being the commonest. 'Playing white' ranges from speaking English in public places outside the classroom, being cloistered with your books at the expense of friendships, being too focussed on good grades, attending schools outside the township, and living in a suburban area instead of a township. Those regarded as 'playing white' may be ostracised, scorned and harassed, even killed as happened to a significant number of people of all ages in different parts of the country during the defiance of the 1980s.

Those who crossed the boundaries were often seen as having betrayed those left behind. They had broken ranks with the group when solidarity meant survival. They were regarded as having endangered everyone's survival. In the poverty-stricken circumstances such as those that prevailed – and still prevail – a problem arises where individual achievement is essential for success. The enormous pressure put on young people not to stand out extracts a huge price. They are caught between the contradictory forces of solidarity and personal achievement.

Bulelani was sophisticated enough to understand the importance of demonstrating to his peers that he was not 'selling out'. His stated position was that he was merely taking advantage of an opportunity to prepare himself so that he could add to the limited township base of tutorial skills could not be faulted. His strategy involved not only keeping in touch with his peers, but nurturing meaningful friendships with some of them. He did not put himself above them. Even though some regarded him as projecting a high and mighty attitude they could not deny his real interest in their own well-being.

Bulelani's case also demonstrates the importance of having caring teachers. His headmaster's support was critical to his acceptance and success at Rhodes High School. The manner in which the headmaster defused the potentially ugly racial conflict by focussing on the similarity of the boys' socioeconomic backgrounds enabled them to empathise with one another. Both boys had fragile egos in a society in which material success was confused with intellectual superiority. Each had to find ways of developing a positive self-image. Bulelani's additional burden of being stigmatised by the colour of his skin had to be transcended.

Without this sort of backing from teachers many township children

TOP: New Crossroads, 1990s.
BOTTOM: Groot Winterhoek Wilderness Area, where some of the weekend trails took place.

TOP & BOTTOM: New Crossroads families.

TOP: Backyard, New Crossroads.
BOTTOM: Fynbos, Cape Point Nature Reserve.

Conversation and solitude which wilderness allows.

Discovering a sense of accomplishment, learning to swim.

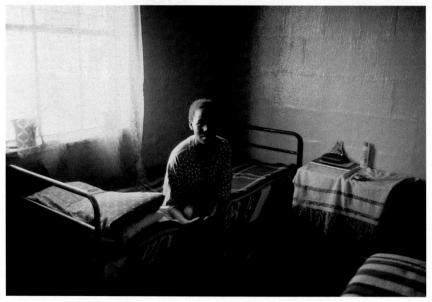

TOP: Freed from the tensions of townhip living, companionship came easily.
BOTTOM: New Crossroads home.

Photo essay by Margot Morrison

flounder. One such person was Tuleka, a conscientious young woman who only started living with both her parents when she was sixteen. Her face reflected the burdens she had had to bear. She looked much older than her years and the corners of her mouth showed the determination with which she tackled every task. She spoke with a deliberate voice, emphasising each syllable.

Tuleka had lived for long periods with her sister in the Transkei, the two of them surviving on their wits. Her parents wanted to protect their children from the violence of the townships in the mid-1980s by keeping them in the rural areas.

TULEKA: School is not totally different [in Transkei] because we read the same books. The only thing is that there was no physical science, no Afrikaans, and no subject offered on a higher grade. My favourite subjects are physical science and mathematics. I want to be a medical doctor like you.

We cope with the overcrowding at home by waiting for everybody to go to sleep, then my sister and I study. There is also a woman who lives two houses down the street from our house who has a little library. She brings books and lends them to us. She also lets us use her library as a study room. When you take a book she makes a record of it to ensure its safe return.

I work hard at school, but I feel that I am not going to do well at the end of the year. We have had too many breaks during the school year. We did not cover all the work prescribed in the curriculum.

Tuleka was worried enough about these disruptions in her schooling to be prepared to repeat Grade 11. She had set her mind on a good career and understood that she would not make it with the level of input she had got from her school up to that point.

In this attitude she was one of those young people who succeeded in completing her high school education against the odds, and despite many setbacks. She eventually registered at a technical college in the Eastern Cape Province, having repeated a few grades mainly because of the teaching disruptions. Tuleka also suffered two nervous breakdowns in 1993 and 1995. She had depression with episodes of acute anxiety – *mafufunyane*, in the local idiom. A spiritual healer helped her through these rough patches, but it was the iron will to succeed that kept her going.

During a workshop I organised to discuss their schooling with the teenagers there were heated debates. Their opinions varied on the need for, and the effectiveness of, school boycotts. Some of them felt that even if boycotts were detrimental to good educational practice, they were effective as a strategy to force the authorities to take note of the problems of inadequate resources in the school system. Others said improvements could be achieved without sacrificing learning time.

LUNGA, THE SON OF A COMMUNITY HEALTH WORKER IN THE TOWNSHIP: *Nangona iischool boycotts zilimosha ixhesha kodwa siyavakala isizathu sazo* – Although school boycotts waste our time, you can understand the reasons for them. We don't have books and there are not enough desks. The problem is that you sit uncomfortably in the classroom the whole day. It affects your ability to listen. Another problem is that teachers assume a lot in the manner in which they teach. At the end of a lesson some say, 'Read this book from page so and so to page so and so at home,' – many pupils don't have books. It wastes time. You cannot blame parents for not having money to buy books because most of our parents are not working. Some parents work for very little money. There is not enough money for books because some books are expensive. I do not disagree with school boycotts.

BULELANI: Most of you like to boycott even if there are books. You can study without textbooks from the teachers' notes. You don't see that time is important. I know, because I went to school at Andile Primary School. I passed without textbooks. The other thing I see about you is that there is no respect among schoolchildren. They do not respect their teachers. They come to class when the teacher is already teaching. Some make a noise. Some are busy smoking. Most of the teachers leave the class because nobody shows any respect for them. This thing of boycotting is something that people do for fun. Although there are good reasons, boycotting is not the answer.

LUNGA: It's a good thing to boycott but we are not doing it in the right way. Even if I have the exam fee that is being demanded to register for the matric at the end of the year now, what will happen to other students next year who don't have it? I must pave the way for other children coming after me. I hear people saying, 'Let us not boycott because the people who say we must boycott have completed their studies a long time ago and they are wasting our time.' That is not true, they do not waste our time. They want us to fix things for ourselves so that things will be better for our children. *Into ndiyikhalazelayo* – what I complain about is the way we engage in boycotts. We are entitled to complain about education, but we should do it in an appropriate way, *nge ndlela ephucukileyo*. It is like a man who saw a fly on the boss's forehead who, in the eagerness to remove the fly, hit his boss. The method is as important as the intention. So we mustn't say we are solving the education crisis and yet we are destroying all education by destroying everything.

There were also pupils like Thabo who saw the boycotts in a very uncomplicated way. Thabo was a likeable young man with an easygoing manner. He was a soccer star on the streets of New Crossroads, famous for his deft tackling and the ability to keep a soccer ball bouncing on his foot for a count of a hundred. He had a wicked sense of humour but was careful not to offend his peers. For him boycotts were an opportunity to do what he liked best. 'It is better not to go to school,' he felt. 'Whenever they say there is no school I just go and play one-armed bandits or soccer. Otherwise it is nice not to go to school.'

Thabo had not managed to get beyond Grade 7. He probably had a learning disability. He could neither read nor write at the Grade 7 level and had repeated most of his grades.

LUNGA: The only problem with boycotting school is the time wasted. We are all getting older. The school results are getting worse. We don't get what we want. We were promised books and only a few arrived. Our classes are as overcrowded as ever. I don't think teachers can manage such large classes. We are not the same – some are clever and others are not so clever.

BULELANI: These school boycotts don't only mean boycotting school but other people's lives are threatened. Cars are stoned for fun. I wish people could be more thoughtful. We must go to school and work rather than sitting down and saying, 'tools down or pens down.' We really need education to succeed in the world today. South Africa needs us with our education. We need to be good examples.

In the toughness of the townships many, understandably, lose their way. Tomela being one. He was born in Old Crossroads in 1978, moved from Cape Town as a baby to stay with his maternal granny because both his parents were working. He was his mother's third, born but his father's second child. The family comprised five boys and a girl, the eldest child having been born when her mother fell pregnant as a teenager. Tomela returned to Cape Town in 1985, but school boycotts delayed his entry into the education system. He was then sent back to the Eastern Cape again.

Tomela was a serious-faced young man with a muscular body. He was attentive in conversations even though he hardly ever initiated them. He had dark, large soft eyes that reflected his sensitive soul and he loved music and enjoyed the hiking trails in the wild. He spent time listening to birdsong and simply being at peace under a shady tree.

Tomela started school in 1986 at Tarkastad in the Eastern Cape Province. Three years later he came back to Cape Town to enter Grade 5 at Walter Teka Primary School in Nyanga. Being a quiet young man, he distanced himself from gangsters, preferring to stay at home listening to music.

TOMELA: I am not at school this year because I could not find a place in any of the schools. They are full. I tried all the schools, but it was already late. They have put me on a waiting list. To be honest, sisi, I did not like the school in Nyanga, because they do not teach well. I wanted the school in Macassar near Khayelitsha. They told us to wait because the school building was still under construction. They promised to open the school in March but they have yet to call us as they promised. My mother went to find out what was happening. She came back and told me that the school was to be opened next year.

My plans are to find another school, but it is late now. I will have to wait for next year. My mother suggested that I must go to Goodwood to learn vocational skills instead of wasting the whole year at home. I told her that is the last thing I want to do. I first want to get my high school diploma then I will take it from there. If I start learning work skills I won't be able to complete school.

My view is to wait for next year unless you can help me find a place in Stembele Matiso High School. My parents had suggested this, but my mother tried but failed to get a place for me.

I then asked him how things were at home.

TOMELA: At home it is alright except that my father always beats me even if I have not done anything wrong. I do not like that. Sometimes I sleep at the homes of friends to run away from him. He hardly buys clothes for me but he buys for other children in the family. He is never satisfied with anything I do. There was a time I wanted to tell you to find a boarding school for me because he is treating me badly.

Each time he comes home he looks for the small mistakes to blame me for. He accuses me of messing up his things. Whenever anything disappears I am the one he blames. He also accuses me of smoking dagga. I'm out of school because there was nobody to accompany me to look for school. My mother only started to help late in the year.

Tomela further refused to enrol for a skills-training course. This is a troubling phenomenon noticeable throughout the country as many black youths associate manual labour with the degrading working conditions their parents had to endure. So careers such as plumbing, electrical contracting, and carpentry are seen as low-status options. Yet for most youths an academic career, no matter how desirable, is not feasible given the poor foundations of their education.

CHAPTER SIX

Community
The essence of humanity is 'our personhood'

I

A sense of belonging is at the heart of being human. Unlike the case with many other members of the animal kingdom, to be human is to be a social being. This is captured in many cultures in different ways. South Africans make much of the uniqueness of ubuntu as an essential tenet of African culture, quoting the expression *umntu ungumtu ngabanye abantu* – a person is only recognised as such through identification with, and by, other people. The essence of this idea is crucial – one's personhood makes sense only in relation to others.

This truism is captured in other cultures as well. Carlo Levi, an Italian artist, writer, and medical doctor, points out that the essence of humanity is our 'personhood' – in other words ubuntu. He defines personhood as 'the meeting place of all our relationships'. Japanese philosophical thought conveys a similar notion in the concept of *amaeru* which represents intimate dependency-relationships.

The focus on personhood or ubuntu is not new. Many classical political texts as well as mythologies capture tensions inherent in the widespread practice in many cultures of subverting the individual will for the common good. Major political dramas depicting how polities and individuals wrestled with this tension have become classics in the film and literary worlds.

The greatest contradiction of being human lies in our individuality having to find expression in the context of being part of the collective. Too much individualism leaves you overly focused on the self and denies you the enrichment that comes from relationships with others. Too much immersion in the group constrains the emergence of the unique talents and creative energies in individuals essential for the enhancement of everyone.

I want to look now at the social context in which young people grow up in New Crossroads. The history of South Africa up to 1994 could be summed up as undermining of the notion of 'belonging' for the indigenous people who constitute the majority of the population. Two major forces were at work here.

Indigenous people were defined as 'other' by colonial settlers. Their exclusion from the common definition of what was human justified the dispossession of the land and opportunities for capital accumulation. The planting of the wild almond hedge by Jan van Riebeeck in 1660, separating settlers from indigenous people, represented a physical and symbolic boundary that was systematically entrenched over the three hundred and fifty years of colonial and apartheid rule. Those regarded as fully human were on one side, while those denied recognition of their humanity found themselves on the other.

This process also denied indigenous people their individuality. They were treated as a collective threat to be managed by direct and indirect rule. Individual talent and creativity were stifled by systematic deprivation and repression. Competition for diminishing resources reduced tolerance levels for individuality and self-expression. The latter were seen as a threat to essential solidarity. A group of ever weaker communities emerged with little regenerative powers from its own talent pool.

The whole apartheid ideology was based on the principle of treating black people as a mass bounded by ethnic groupings best managed by divide-and-rule politics. The individuality of black people was submerged in a collective which was defined by racism. Cecil John Rhodes put it bluntly in 1888: 'We are to be lords over them and let them be a subject race.'

New Crossroads's history reflects the impact of this legacy. As the stories have shown, many men and women in the township felt helpless to provide for their children and opted out in self-defence. This decision by many poor men to shed family responsibilities left little room for young men to model themselves on successful males. Conflict between the ideals of a patriarchal system which installs the male as provider, protector and decision-maker on one hand, and the harsh realities of lack of education and skills, compounded by high levels of unemployment and demoralisation on the other, leave young men confused. They lack the father model with the tools to assume the authority and responsibility of being male in a patriarchal society. To all intents and purposes many young people were abandoned by their fathers and left to find their own path into adulthood.

The ability of communities to deal with periods of hardship or rapid change is often determined by the ways in which they react to both ongoing stresses and traumatic events. South Africa's past neglect of public policies and the present lack of capacity by the government to implement its progressive policies continue to put a strain on communities on the edge of survival.

Jewish people have been singularly successful in dealing with periods of hardship and traumatic events throughout their history, often against the odds. The focus on education as the route out of poverty and a source of wisdom has enriched this community. Their high skill levels make them indispensable across the globe. The promotion of individual talents and pressure on achievement has created, over generations, a fiercely competitive people. Even though they may be a minority in many parts of the world, they have been able to hold their own. The reverence for their cultural heritage is the glue that binds them together to provide the necessary support against external threats. Solidarity is finely balanced with a celebration of individual aspirations and achievements.

It is not insignificant that Jewish culture has a long history and tradition of literacy and respect for the scientific method. As the writer and thinker Edward Wilson says of the importance of a science culture, 'Without the instruments and accumulated knowledge of the natural sciences – physics, chemistry and biology – human beings are trapped in a cognitive prison. They are like intelligent fish born in a deep, shadowed pool. Wondering and restless, longing to reach out, they think about the world outside.'

Jewish culture not only possesses the instruments and the accumulated knowledge of the natural sciences, but it celebrates and promotes excellence in those individuals engaged in scientific work. It has also harmonised the world of science with that of a larger purpose and created what Wilson calls a 'sacred narrative' that links them to their ancestors and a creator.

The ways disempowered black communities have responded to colonialism and apartheid stand in stark contrast to the Jewish experience. The lack of depth in the literary and scientific traditions of most African cultures has left many in a cognitive prison. Of course, the deliberate denial of educational opportunities to African people has undermined the basis for the rapid development of a science culture. Innate intelligence is no substitute for accumulated knowledge and access to the instruments of scientific enquiry essential to living in a modern world.

There is a joke in township parlance that compares and contrasts African and Jewish cultures with respect to support for individual success. Jewish people are said to have a tradition that holds up the ladder of success to individuals to climb out of poverty, knowing that once such individuals succeed they will pull up the rest of the community. Africans, in contrast, are said to be hampered by mistrust. Although they may initially hold up the ladder, as soon as the individual reaches the upper levels, they start doubting the wisdom of their action: what if the individual reaches the top and forgets about them? They are then apt to pull the ladder away and let the individual come crashing down. A variation on the same theme of mistrust occurs in those cases where the community keeps its side of the bargain, but the successful individual leaves the rest stranded below.

II

Despite the tensions that inevitably occur between households in poverty-stricken communities, co-operation remains necessary because of the low levels of essential services. Sharing is often the only way of ensuring access to resources. So households share toilets and water taps. A more recent, and dangerous, development is the sharing of electricity between households through electrical connections illegally tapped into the supply lines. Some of these connections break every safety rule in the book: live wires crossing streets, disconnected trip switches and deactivated power monitors. Obviously no local government anywhere in the world can afford to cater for communities with an entrenched culture of non-payment or illegal usage, yet this culture is alive and well in New Crossroads.

Nor is this situation sustainable between households. Stress in poor communities mitigates against it as people have to strike a delicate balance between their own household needs and good relations with those with whom they share resources.

Jealousy and envy between households is a common feature of community life in New Crossroads. Levels of trust are strongly linked to the availability of adequate basic resources. It is in the competition for these resources that the gap between the ideals that people live by and the reality that they live with is most pronounced. By focussing on community priorities people have to set their horizons beyond their immediate familial or personal needs. This inevitably creates tensions, as some of the stories have already shown.

I came across it, too, in Tuleka's family. Her family had a close relationship with a neighbouring family. The two households – a total of eighteen people – acted as one, almost merging and losing their individual identities. Tuleka's family consisted of her parents and four siblings, her uncle, his wife and three children and another extended family member. Their neighbours were a nuclear family with four children.

The children could choose to sleep in either home; they wore one another's clothes, and shared their meals. Tuleka's family was the poorer of the two, with a household income of R1 000. The other family ran a taxi business and had almost three times Tuleka's household's disposable income.

The better-off children began to resent sharing their material possessions with Tuleka's family. Ridicule and gossip replaced intimacy amongst the children. The crunch came when Tuleka's cousin was insulted and assaulted by the neighbour's children at school. She came home with a chunk of her hair torn out and her school uniform in shreds.

Tuleka and her elder sister went to avenge their cousin's humiliation. A free-for-all broke out. Parents and children joined in the fight. The woman in the other family tried to stab Tuleka's mother with a broken bottle but she tripped and fell on it and cut her face badly. Tuleka was proud that her family was the stronger of the two and routed the other side. Their physical strength and courage in battle made up for their material poverty. They were able to redeem their self-esteem.

A merger of households is difficult to sustain under the best of circumstances. In Tuleka's instance the odds were strongly against sustainability. The gross inequalities in the reciprocal relationship made one household a donor and the other a recipient with all the complexities of such a relationship. Over time the receiver starts resenting the giver. There is also the humiliation which poverty visits upon its victims. Self-esteem is often low and oversensitivity to any suggestion of indignity is likely to invoke a strong response. Another common feature of New Crossroads is jealousy between neighbours.

LUNGA'S MOTHER, MRS MDE: The kids here are very curious to know how I get money to send my kids to school. Bobokazi is also at a white school – all my kids go to coloured schools or white schools. There's a lot of jealousy here.

BULELWA: Even in my neighbourhood it's the same. There's a lot of jealousy here. We had the same thing in our street, with one family influencing other families. We talked for years and years trying to resolve the problem until mum eventually reached saturation point. We were sitting in our home when the neighbours came and started swearing at us. We went out and got objects with which to hit them. We got out of the gate and whipped them.

MRS MDE: These people have been giving my family a hard time. Two weeks ago we had to fight. It starts with the kids and then it goes to the parents. When you want an explanation of misconduct from children the parents are ready for a showdown. It's jealousy.

BULELWA: We even had a community meeting about our own problems with neighbours, but could not get to the bottom of what the conflict was about. It was just jealousy.

Jealousy or envy is a recurring theme. Those with some means of support are envied by those without and expected to share the little they have. Mrs Mde is the local community health worker – a position that enables her to have a regular source of income as well as to be of service to fellow members of the community. Her services are appreciated, but the ambivalence remains. Why must she be so lucky to have a job when others have to live in grinding poverty?

Similarly, that Bulelwa or any other young person can afford to go to a better school is seen as having taken away opportunities from others. It is a vicious circle and there is palpable discomfort in this community with the growing class distinctions as social mobility opportunities open up.

Bulelwa has spoken of being regarded as being 'high and mighty' by her neighbours. She said that the other children in their street did not like her family. They resented Bulelwa and her sisters for not engaging in sexual liaisons or drinking. Their behaviour was seen as an indication that the Leseka girls thought themselves to be superior. In response the neighbours taunted them continually and threw objects at them across the fence into their property. As she also pointed out, it was the same fear of jealousy that motivated Bulelwa to get married in Port Elizabeth. She was convinced that such an occasion would provoke envy among people in New Crossroads. It is a sad irony that a community could be reduced to not celebrating the success of its own children because of too much pain from too many failures.

Given these considerations, highly successful individuals tend to migrate elsewhere. Both Bulelwa and her sister's families live outside New Crossroads in a neighbourhood that gives them the space to be themselves and to celebrate their successes. Many other professionals have also moved in search of greener pastures. New Crossroads is consequently deprived of positive role models and potential innovators.

Bulelani's narrative shows further aspects of an unhappiness with township life. He spoke of being a loner. 'I do not trust anyone on this earth. Most of the time I want to be alone,' he told me. It may have been this loner quality that enabled him to push ahead while others in a similar position have opted to stay with the herd. Bulelani's loner status is partly a protective device against the excessive demands of a group that does not tolerate individuality, but also allows him to pursue his own interests. The cost, though, is happiness.

BULELANI: I am not happy. I don't go to anyone when I have a problem. I can't identify what my problem is. I don't know how to describe it, but I am not happy at all. Even when I am with friends I am happy for a short time but then I start feeling the pain again. I like having friends but they are no help to me in any way. So I don't think I am happy at all. That is why I like to be alone. I try to play games with other people but I always say, 'No, I am not going to make it,' and I drop it. I always have to find a place to be alone.

III

Some of the processes at play in the lives of Bulelwa and Bulelani reflect the inevitable class boundaries that accompany the move from traditional society to modernity.

Bulelani feels like an outsider in New Crossroads. He feels different. He tries to conform but that does not seem to work for him. He feels trapped.

Aggravating the situation is a history that has told African people they are inferior and has led to a condition sociologists refer to as 'learned helplessness'. This has affected white people too. How else can one explain why it took so long for the voting white public to realise that apartheid was not only bankrupt politically, socially and economically, but also unsustainable in a modern world? The authoritarian culture that enveloped much of apartheid South Africa encouraged learned helplessness and an overreliance on authority to make all the important political and social decisions.

In individual and group interviews with the adolescents and their families I came across a sense of helplessness. Many families whose histories have been marked by titanic struggles for survival reach a point of physical and mental exhaustion. Many of them have, over a long period, put effort into improving their lot with little return on that investment. Some of the teenagers had themselves reached dangerous levels of despair. Even though Bulelani felt alone, many others shared the despair he experienced.

For example, Tuleka became psychologically unbalanced. She developed a condition known as *mafufunyane* that responded to spiritual healing by a local charismatic pastor. This condition is characterised by periods of panic-anxiety with loss of control over one's actions followed by spells of depression. *Mafufunyane* is believed to be brought about by evil spirits introduced into you by envious people. Almost all the families interviewed were either experiencing or had experienced the pain of having a member of the family with psychological problems.

The cruel irony was that there wasn't a single psychological service within easy access of the New Crossroads community. Not surprisingly a lot of reliance was placed on traditional and spiritual healers who shared the life of the community.

The benefits derived from traditional and spiritual healing have to be seen in the context of the risks of reinforcing the tendency to learned helplessness. Placing the cause of problems on evil forces or spirits and invoking supernatural powers reduces anxiety and guilt in the short and medium term but it doesn't identify, analyse and solve the problems.

IV

The history of communal action in New Crossroads has not always been a positive one. After the leadership of Old Crossroads entered into negotiations with the apartheid government in the late 1970s, the government effectively used divide-and-rule tactics to turn different warlord-led factions against each other. Residents were forced to choose sides or suffer the consequences.

MRS XABA: We came to Cape Town in 1976. My husband paid lobola. We lived in Old Crossroads. At first in Old Crossroads my life with my husband was nice and smooth. Then started the problem of the war between the two main leaders, Memani and Ngxobongwana, and the police.

Life was very difficult. For us it was better because my husband was working. In 1980 I fell pregnant. It was very bad because we had to run and sleep under trees.

Groups of different leaders were fighting each other. The war cry was: *Amadoda phandle, abafazi endlwini* – men come outside, women must stay indoors. Ngxobongwana's men wore white head-dresses to distinguish themselves from others in battle. The other group tied strips of yellow fabric around their legs.

I was very young and inexperienced. I was frightened. I would not let my husband join the battles. So I hid him under me and slept on top of him and covered both of us with blankets. The men came inside and looked under the bed. They did not find him. He was suffocating under my weight but had to steel himself.

Mrs Yantolo's story from those years is typical.

MRS YANTOLO: In 1977 my husband took me. We got married. We stayed in Old Crossroads with his father's younger brother, *tatomncinci* [literally, little father]. While we stayed in Old Crossroads waiting for our rights, the *amabhulu* said that we should move away completely because they wanted the bush. Be! We just stayed. We said we were not going anywhere. The boers came with dogs. They chased the people. I remember that at this time I was pregnant with this Mpumi. I said, 'Eyi! I am struggling with always having to sleep outside.' I remember we were sleeping in the bush, pregnant as I was.

We built our *tenti* in the bush. The boers chased us at night. We were beaten. If a boer met you hiding he would kick you and pass by and chase the men. It went on like this without us sleeping deeply. I gave birth to Mpumi during the sixth month of pregnancy. I thought it was a miscarriage because I was not expecting her at that time. My husband and I walked to Somerset Hospital where Mpumi was born. She was kept in hospital until she grew big enough to be taken home.

As time went on I could see the people who were looking after us or leading us were divided. They began to clash. The boer's war ended and we started our own war. The table was cracked in the middle. Some supported Memane, others, Ngxobongwana. There was a lot of beating. You did not know when it would be your turn to be beaten. We beat one another. There was fighting in Old Crossroads and it was very painful. People ran away and left their houses. The shacks were on fire.

When we arrived in Old Crossroads we built a new *tenti* in Section Four. It was unfortunate that we had three children under those conditions. On the 28th February 1982, on a Saturday, our shack was burnt. We did not know what had caused the fire. Our children were saved because I was there. I had just come back from having an appendix operation at Somerset Hospital. I was discharged on a Thursday. The shack was burnt on the Saturday. A person who was staying with us died inside.

I took the children out through the window because it was burning in the kitchen. There was no way we could get out through the door. We were the last people to get out. The children were in their nightclothes. I threw them out of the window and I followed. While I was throwing them out of the window, Mpumi was nervous. She went back inside the house. She did not know what she was doing. When I jumped outside I noticed that Mpumi was not with the other children. Luckily, in the light of the fire, I saw Mpumi inside the house running around. I threw myself inside. I just threw the other two whom I had by the hand outside and grabbed Mpumi. While I was inside Nana cried that I should take her. Philani was only six months old. I managed to get the three of them out of danger.

I sat down. Then my mind came back. 'That is my shack that is burning,' and I realised that my children were in front of me. My husband was not there because he was the first person who got out. Luckily he thought about us and found us safe.

We came back and went to Nontsumpa's [the township superintendent's] office on a Monday. We wanted a house in New Crossroads because I wouldn't build in Old Crossroads anymore. That was the third shack which was burnt and that had to be the last because a human being had died there. It was sad because we did not have a place to bury the person. We asked the neighbours to help us because we did not have a place to bury him because our shack was burnt.

Dasoyi refused to give us a house. He said that he did not have any houses. I said I would not build a shack anywhere again. I only wanted a house in New Crossroads. Dasoyi said, 'There are no houses at New Crossroads.' I said, 'There are.' He said, 'Do you want to do my job for me? Come and sit at my desk and do my job because I am telling you there are no houses and you say there are. Take my job.' I kept quiet. I saw that this worked on Dasoyi's mind. Later he gave me a key and a house number.

We stayed in that empty house with nothing. I was attacked by nerves (I fell into a depression) because I thought that everything I had was going wrong. I wasn't working. My husband was working alone. People gave us household effects including children's clothes. We lived on the charity of neighbours. Eventually I found a job. We stayed in that hall [empty house]. We did not have a thing.

V

As I have pointed out, strife and power games characterised the emergence of New Crossroads. The legacy of the divide-and-rule tactics to maintain white privilege had eroded trust relationships within this community. In addition, the authoritarian nature of apartheid rule promoted authoritarian social relationships. The very people fighting for liberation from oppressive white rule adopted the same authoritarian approach to leadership and social relationships. Debate and expression of differences of opinion were discouraged. Loyalty to leaders was extracted through the threat or actual use of force.

Violence became, and remains, a means of enforcing compliance with the wishes of the powerful. South Africa is sadly riddled with a culture of violence. Tom Lodge, a political scientist at the University of the Witwatersrand, made an apt comment on the nature of this violence when he wrote: 'What makes politics for many South Africans a matter of life and death is not a set of false fears or unreasonable prejudices. Politics is murderous because the stakes involved in who wins or who loses concern matters which affect people's lives in the most essential ways.'

The stakes may look very low to outsiders. Yet the right to erect a shack on some polluted piece of ground spelt the difference between having an urban home or returning to a bleak future in the rural areas.

Young people growing up in New Crossroads are embroiled in this culture of violence. They have few role models they can rely on to guide their personal development. They are left to find their own way, and turn to their peers. Such peer groups tend to reflect the authoritarian culture of their societies. It is not surprising that gang activity is so rife.

Many of the parents of the children in my project regarded peer relations with suspicion. They perceived their children as spending too much time with peers instead of pursuing 'useful tasks'. Most

113

parents saw their children's friends as a potential source of values and practices which were at variance with their own, as well as those they desired for their children. A common refrain was: 'The street has its own school which is in competition with what we teach children at home.'

Such concerns seem to be universal, although research suggests that adolescents are likely to follow adult advice in matters pertaining to their long-term future. Their friends are used mainly in matters of short-term concern. However, it seems that adolescent choices in such cases depend on their perception of who is likely to follow up on the outcome of their choice. If adolescents feel that their parents take enough interest in them, and follow up with support and encouragement, they are more likely to choose the advice of their parents.

With only a few exceptions, the adolescents on the project had poor communications with their parents. Lunga was emphatic about the need to keep parents in the dark – 'we must not bring things to them, they are cruel.' Others simply ignored their parents as sources of advice because of a perceived lack of empathy. Parents were also seen as being too busy to talk about relevant issues. As I've pointed out, the relentless demands of the need to provide for urgently needed material resources left parents with little time to focus on emotional support for their offspring. In such cases, peers and friends become the only support and authorities.

There were also numerous complaints about bullying by peers in the streets. This particularly affected those adolescents seen to be vulnerable, in other words who didn't have the protection of a 'big brother'.

Xola, one of the group of sixteen, put it this way: 'There are older boys in the street who beat us. At times they want money and they will beat us if we don't have any. Or if an older person sends a boy to the shop, that boy will ask one of our group to go to the shop instead. If we refuse to go, we get beaten.'

Mthetheleli, who lived on the same street as Xola, had resorted to playing with children younger than himself because 'they are less troublesome than my own peers'. He also relied on his father's reputation for beating up those who offended him to keep the bullyboys away.

Street life in the townships does not respect tidy boundaries. Peer group activity sometimes slides into gangsterism. Adolescents hanging around become bored and are drawn into more exciting vistas: bullying, harassment of others, 'forced sharing of scarce resource', 'repossession', and open violence which may result in loss of life. 'Forced sharing' and 'repossession' are politically charged and legitimated metaphors for stealing or robbing someone perceived to have more resources than yourself. Territoriality also seems to be a major underlying cause of disputes. Finding yourself on the wrong side of an invisible territorial boundary could have a high cost. The increasingly common tendency towards a violent settlement of disputes reflects an entrenched social culture of structural and physical violence.

During the gang troubles of the early nineties the approach used by community leaders to stop gang activity in New Crossroads was to beat up any young men found wandering around the streets after dark. If you did not want to get beaten up, you spent the evening at home. A great deal of pressure was put on families whose children were known to be involved in gangs. They either had to cast out their sons or the community would force these boys to leave the township. This approach was, by all accounts, successful in ridding New Crossroads of gangs in the early 1990s.

The success of this attitude depended to a large extent on a community that was prepared to submerge even parental self-interest to fight together to banish any criminal activity. However, this success cannot only be attributed to the community pulling together (as the New Crossroads residents like to represent it). The brutal and ruthless means employed by the men terrorised active and potential gangsters enough to force them off the streets.

Gangsterism however reared its head again in New Crossroads in the late 1990s. Some residents tried to use the old tactics to purge the township of gangs. However, this time conditions had changed. The combined efforts of some residents of New Crossroads and the Community Policing Forum to call communal meetings in an attempt to bring together both the young boys involved in gang violence and their parents yielded little results. The Community Policing Forum also held public displays of weapons captured from various households in New Crossroads in an attempt to shock people into realising the magnitude of the problem. They hoped in vain to get the community to take responsibility for tackling this problem.

The New Crossroads Community Policing Forum was set up in 1996 to boost the policing services in this township. The Policing Forum is based at a temporary police station within the Community Centre. The young people I spoke to expressed profound scepticism about the value of these meetings and the likelihood that they would be well attended. There also seemed to be little faith in the Community Policing Forum as a structure. Policing in New Crossroads is officially under the jurisdiction of the Nyanga Police Station which is seriously under-resourced.

In one interview the youngster and the researcher couldn't suppress their giggles when they mentioned the Community Policing Forum: 'It's the Police Forum. They're quite funny. They can't put an end to violence. The youngsters are not scared of them because they are carrying guns themselves. So the Police Forum is quiet. They are trying their best but they are ineffectual.'

'They need school.'

'Shame, they just got the job. None of them went for training or anything.'

The policing system in New Crossroads seems hopelessly under-resourced and ill-equipped. This system might work in a small, close-knit, unarmed rural community but it is highly inadequate to the task in contemporary New Crossroads where there is widespread disillusionment with police effectiveness and the ability of the criminal justice structures to deal with crime. The predominant perception is that criminals have far more power than the police. Life is tough. It is a case of each for him- or herself. No one, including the police, seems able to offer protection.

Pule, who'd been abandoned by her mother and brought up by her grandmother, knew well the reality of street life.

PULE: I was almost raped. I was attacked by boys who are known to me. They live round here in the same street. They were joined by their friends who live in other areas. I was rescued by a guy who spent time

116

in jail. Those people are very rough – they've just come out of jail. The guy who rescued me negotiated with those guys in jail language so they understood him. They let me go. I went to lay a charge but I didn't go to the police station. I went to the guy who is the caretaker at the Youth Centre – he's on the Community Policing Forum – but he didn't take it any further.

Later it emerged that the caretaker had not taken the charge any further because Pule had become scared of pressing charges. Her attackers had not given her any trouble since. But she still lived in fear.

PULE: I'm really scared of them. All of them now have guns. They even shoot old people. I heard that they raped a pregnant girl in another area. The leaders of this gang are three guys. They are the ones responsible for the township fight between Guguletu and New Crossroads. They are not scared of the police. The Policing Forum can do nothing to them – they shoot back. NY53 and NY57 are the most violent areas – you can't go there after 5 p.m. The guys from KTC are also involved – they are helping the New Crossroads guys.

Lawlessness and helplessness are the order of the day in New Crossroads in the post-apartheid era. The criminal justice system has yet to adapt to enforcing the law under the Constitutional requirements of a human-rights culture. There seems to be an approach to err on the side of respecting the rights of criminals even if these rights infringe those of law-abiding citizens. Poor training and under-resourcing add to the inefficiencies and ineffectualness of the criminal justice system. Residents feel vulnerable to the criminals around them, including their own children over whom they have lost control. It is a jungle life.

Many years after Phalo was killed by his friends I visited his parents but they still had not heard from the police about how the case was progressing. They were resigned to waiting. They also mentioned that one of Phalo's friends was using his name in committing crimes. This resulted in numerous phone calls from various people demanding to speak to Phalo about crimes committed in his name. Phalo's parents felt powerless to do anything about it. They knew the suspects in the murder of their son, but they had no way of insisting that the law-enforcement system brought them to book. They also feared reprisals given the inefficiency of the police in protecting complainants in criminal cases.

With this lack of faith in the police and frustration at rising crime levels I started hearing stories about street justice. In fact, a member of the New Crossroads Community Policing Forum told me about two young boys caught stealing from a taxi driver. A group of 'taxi men' got together and kidnapped the two boys. They beat them up severely. Two days later, the boys had not yet returned home. Their parents went to the 'taxi men' and asked for their sons. It is ironic that the parents went to the 'taxi men' in this instance and not to the police. When the story was related to me both boys were in hospital in a critical condition. I heard the following day one of them had died. The second had a fractured skull. It was not clear that he would survive.

What was most disturbing about this story was the underlying acceptance of mob justice as a legitimate response to the high level of criminal activity. The story was told to demonstrate that, although crime was high in New Crossroads, residents were determined to deal harshly with criminals. There was little sympathy for the boys, although I was told that it was unfortunate that this incident had occurred. The main message seemed to be that the boys were silly to have messed with the wrong people. There was acceptance that the punishment they received was justified. If people played with fire they had themselves to blame should they burn.

There have been a host of similar cases of civilians taking the law into their own hands and of anger at ineffectual policing and widespread corruption and involvement in criminal activities in the police ranks.

While the public may have every reason to take the law into its own hands, vigilantism not only undermines the justice system but is likely to entrench arbitrary justice based on individual discretion or small interest groups. The Nigerian Nobel laureate, Wole Soyinka, writes of 'the injustices that often accompany [the] righteous thirst for justice'. People living in townships such as New Crossroads thirst in vain for justice in the new South Africa.

Many residents of Crossroads recall the harrowing experiences of mob justice in the early 1980s when victims were often indiscriminately selected. A report into the violence found that in the atmosphere of fear and suspicion 'anyone who was in the wrong place at the wrong time, or lived in the wrong area, was open to attack from an opposing group. There were very few, if any, neutral or safe areas within and around Crossroads.'

One of the results of the high level of violence in New Crossroads is that it severely restricts public space. On one occasion fighting between two groups of young boys from Guguletu and New Crossroads reduced access to two main roads in New Crossroads in the evenings, one of the roads being the main link to the train station. 'Every day they start fighting at 5 p.m.,' I was told. 'Even old people are warned not to use this route to the train station. Two boys from New Crossroads and one from Guguletu were killed in this fighting.'

Pule, who lives in a particularly dangerous area of New Crossroads, says that people padlocked themselves in their houses at night. The Youth Centre in New Crossroads, built as part of the research project to provide local youth with a resource to offer them skills, entertainment and education, was under-utilised because people were afraid to use it. It was located in a gang-infested quarter and there had been several rapes in areas adjacent to the Centre. It was a cruel irony that a facility intended to address a pressing need became inaccessible because the problem of youth crime was larger than the community could handle. Most of the young people in our project said they would not go to the Youth Centre because it was too dangerous.

DUMO, THE QUIET ONE: It's violent there. People shoot each other. They need to get involved in more positive activities. The Centre was built for them and that's exactly where they live. There should be more workshops there – there should be more involvement. The Centre is exactly in that area. I don't think the Centre can work well if people are going there carrying guns.

I have enemies there in the Centre. That guy, the tall one who plays basketball. They wanted to kill me the other day. I don't like the violence in New Crossroads – especially in the area around the Centre.

There are rapists near the Centre – some of them used to stay there. I'm afraid to go that side because it's dangerous, especially for girls.

The levels of crime and violence in New Crossroads seem cyclical. There is a crying need for more community facilities. Recreational facilities, particularly for youth, are vital to normal development. The government's 1994 Reconstruction and Development Programme report setting the scene for the post-apartheid development thrust noted that: 'One of the cruellest legacies of apartheid is its distortion of sports and recreation in South Africa. It has denied millions of people, especially the youth, a normal and healthy society.'

Many young people move out of Cape Town to escape the violence and the danger of being recruited by gangs. A newspaper editorial noted the irony of children being sent out of Cape Town to avoid violence whereas in the past many were sent to Cape Town for their safety. A significant number of the young people in my project were sent back to relatives in the Ciskei or the Transkei whenever boycotts and fighting in Cape Town made schooling and living unsafe.

There is often intense pressure to join gangs, as the grandmother of a boy sent to Pretoria to avoid the gangs explained: 'If you are a young man and not involved in the gangs you are attacked. If they think you have associations with gang members, you are attacked. If they think your son is a gang member you are attacked.'

Bulelani had joined a gang by default, and Lunga had a similar experience.

LUNGA: I also found myself being a member of a gang without realising what was happening. My story is the same as Bulelani's. One day I went to Nyanga. I met a group of people. I was in a bad situation in Nyanga because they said I was a Badboy from New Crossroads. I didn't want to get involved in a fight. I didn't want to do anything wrong. But those people can make you fight even if you are not prepared to do so. It took me a long time to go to Nyanga again. The only thing was that if someone from Nyanga or Guguletu was in New Crossroads, I would help to beat them. In Guguletu and Nyanga, when you come from New Crossroads they beat you because they assume that you must be a member of the Badboys.

Another youngster, Tumi, had two brothers involved in rival gangs. Her mother eventually sent one of them away to her brother in the

Transkei because she feared that they would eventually kill each other. Such was the level of violence that it respected no familial bonds or brotherly obligations.

Mthetheleli, also had to be sent to the Transkei to 'escape this life, township life. My friends are all smoking and drinking. I wanted to leave this lifestyle before I got affected.'

Bulelani suggested in a conversation about this problem that the only effective way to stop the problem of gangs in New Crossroads was to take some of the children involved outside the township and expose them to an alternative reality. He believed strongly that they needed to experience different options in social relationships. In his analysis they were sweet boys who had been sucked into a destructive lifestyle but given the chance they might have been able to rethink their behaviour. As he put it: 'Life for them is getting out of hand.' Indeed on many occasions at the end of our weekend wilderness trails, some of the young people pleaded that we should just stay in those areas to give them a chance to live a higher quality life.

BULELANI: These guys need to be taken out of their environment and learn to live as people and appreciate who they are. Some of them are from difficult backgrounds. Their anger from home goes straight out onto the streets. We need to find ways of keeping these boys involved and to explain to them what life's about.

If I had grown up and not allowed myself to be tamed by my parents I'd also be abusing alcohol and guns. These conflicts initially took place under the influence of alcohol. I know these boys – they are sweet boys when they're sober – now two or three of them are dead already. Some of them I know. It's not nice to see small boys dead.

I have a dream that the youth who are violent will come back into the fold of humanity. Life for them is getting out of hand. If we don't act now there will be problems. They are even fighting with their parents – shouting back and affecting other people who have done nothing.

Most of them don't go to school. Some of them would like to go back but they are afraid because they are involved in gangs. Gangsterism is not something we can live with – this has been proved. They are not the first to get into gangsterism. It's been proved you can't grow up normal if you get involved in that way of life. Once you kill one you kill more.

VII

Bulelani raised the question about how much the environment actually influenced a person. The view that New Crossroads was so bad that the only way of avoiding its influence was to move away carried credence among many other residents. The same applied to other troubled townships in the Western Cape. People were giving up on them.

There is a real danger that in the long term New Crossroads and other townships will become stigmatised areas that people will abandon in greater numbers. Successful residents who are able to work themselves out of the poverty trap are likely to escape the township as soon as they can. Those who are left behind will have increasingly fewer resources at their disposal. What little there is will be further diminished by the flight of positive role models. Spatial apartheid is likely to continue under these circumstances – one more example of the past holding the future to ransom.

The Chairperson of the Guguletu Policing Forum, Mr Landingwe, argued some years ago that parents sending their children out of the townships to avoid trouble were doing nothing to solve the problem. 'By sending children away to avoid bad influences, they are ducking the problem. Bad influences are everywhere.' He felt that many of the children being sent away were actually still involved in gang activities, although their parents were unaware of this. 'Parents have become relaxed about giving guidance to their children. As a result we have gang problems. Parents need to take control,' he said.

Mr Landingwe's analysis of the situation, logical as it is, is cold comfort to parents whose children's lives are in danger in a real sense. What kind of parent is likely to make her/his child a sacrificial lamb to strengthen a community at war with itself and its future? Residents of these impoverished townships seem to be in a no-win situation. They know what needs to be done in many cases, but lack the capacity to do it. The future is too remote when everyday existence is such a struggle.

CHAPTER SEVEN

A development intervention
'We will learn there, we will play there'

I

How do you intervene in the lives of young people within as complex a context as that of New Crossroads? Can an outsider help reconfigure their living environment in a manner that lowers the risks facing young people? Is successful development intervention possible in a context in which the level of 'common wealth' is so dangerously low? What risks should you be alert to in tackling such a challenge? How do you lower the risk of failure? These were the questions constantly in my mind during this project.

Two forces inspired the project to incorporate an 'intervention element'. The first was idealism. I am an unreconstructed idealist. I firmly believe in the capacity of human beings to transcend the constraints of their circumstances and dare to imagine a different future. My personal life has reinforced my idealism. Given sufficient support human beings can defy the odds and become agents of history.

The second guiding tenet was the strong objection expressed by the New Crossroads community to being used as the subjects of a project without deriving any tangible benefits. I embarked on this project confident that there would be enough momentum generated by these two forces to sustain the efforts of those involved in planning an appropriate undertaking to make a success of it.

The venture was launched after protracted negotiations with the New Crossroads Civic Association, one of the many grassroots organisations of township residents which sprang up in the dying stages of apartheid as part of the United Democratic Front. (While the ANC was banned the UDF promoted its objectives, but was disbanded in the early 1990s with the ANC's unbanning.)

My historical ties with the Black Consciousness Movement as one of its founder members in the 1970s, were viewed with suspicion by many Civic Association leaders. They feared that the venture would give me a political base to challenge the ANC's predominant position in the township.

The publicly stated non-aligned political status I was committed to was insufficient reassurance to sceptics. People in this environment did not believe that it was possible to be an activist without affiliation to a political party. Nor did my friendship with many of the ANC's top leaders convince them of my non-partisanship. If anything, some of the activists were suspicious of my motivation for befriending their leaders but not becoming a card-carrying party member. My reasons for not participating in party politics centred on my knowledge of the political terrain which tolerated nothing short of total loyalty to the party line even when such a line made no sense in terms of public policy. I have always seen my role as a change agent working with poor communities wherever they were to be found, regardless of their political views. The freedom to engage with people regardless of their political affiliation is at the heart of social transformation. Party politics is a fickle thing – here today, gone tomorrow. Social transformation is a dynamic that accompanies history throughout the ages. It took patience to keep negotiations on track and finally to win the approval of the majority in New Crossroads.

II

At a special forum of residents called by the Civic Association, constructing a youth centre was seen as the most appropriate venture to address the problems facing young people living in New Crossroads and surrounding townships. A memorandum of understanding was drawn up after the meeting with input from all sectors of the resident population, young and old, men and women, members of different political organisations as well as non-aligned people. The key points were that the Youth Centre would be a resource for all children of New Crossroads regardless of political affiliation, and a safe place for learning and recreation. The community committed themselves to actively supporting and maintaining the Centre. They were to have a say in design and construction, and would fund part of the cost through voluntary household-based contributions.

But it was the children and young people's forum that graphically captured the vision of the Youth Centre: 'We want a place where we can learn karate and dancing. We want a library where we can read books. We want advice on how to lead our lives. We want to learn computer games like white children.'

What has become of these dreams? Turning ideals into reality in this environment entailed much more than I had bargained for.

After the agreement it took another two years before there was consensus on a site. Having initially allocated a site at the heart of New Crossroads near two major schools and a crèche, the Civic Association, under the influence of its chairman, reneged. Plans for a proposed community centre modelled on Cape Town's Good Hope Centre included the use of the entire block of the earmarked land. Objections by some members of the community to a building of such an elaborate structure, which had proven unworkable even in the hands of a well-endowed Cape Town City Council, were brushed aside. The Youth Centre was then allocated land towards the edge of New Crossroads near the KTC squatter camp.

The proposed location of the Youth Centre left many of the dedicated parents of my project deeply perturbed. They knew the area to be crime ridden. They were quite emphatic that the site was unsuitable for the agreed objectives. But they lost the argument at community meetings. We were in a weak position to enforce any choice on the community which was dominated by the chair of the Civic Association who had political clout both inside and outside the township. Community ownership of development initiatives includes ownership of mistakes and risks. However bitter the pill, it has to be swallowed once attempts to point to better alternatives have failed. Our role was to give support and advice but not to dictate the terms of engagement. Yet the land allocation decision would have major negative implications for the ability of the Youth Centre to attain its set objectives.

Follow-up workshops were conducted by my research assistants to clarify the vision, expectations and responsibilities of all parties. At one of the initial workshops attended by some one hundred and sixty-seven children between the ages of ten and fourteen the enthusiasm was audible, palpable and visible. The children composed songs with the encouragement of the researchers:

Sifuna ukwakha isakhiwo solutsha (We want to build a building for the youth)
Siza kuba sisakhiwo sethu (It is going to be our building)
siza kufunda khona (We will learn there)
siza kufunda (We will learn)
siza kudlala khona (We will play there)
siza kudlala (We will play)
siza kukhulela khona (We will grow there)
siza kukhula. (We will grow.)

This song of hope and optimism about the future of young people with a Centre of their own was adopted by all and sung with great energy. It was complemented by other expressions of hope. With the assistance of the architect, the children made sketches of what the Centre could look like. They committed their dreams to paper and were asked to explore a room in the proposed design. They then role-played what each room or space could be used for. At the end of the morning they reported back to the forum about their ideas for use of the space.

Two examples:

'We talked about the music room. We will need musical instruments. We will need a piano, guitars and other things. When we come back from school in the afternoons we want to learn music.'

'We are the youth leaders. We were in the office. People coming to the Centre should come in with yellow membership cards which they must show at the gate. We will have a computer for typing so that people who want to learn how to use computers can have lessons on Saturdays. The use of any equipment should be authorised by elected leaders. The leaders will be responsible for organising holiday projects and fundraising.'

At the end of the day thirty-three a few of the oldest children were selected for a workshop to make clay face masks to hang in the proposed Centre. This workshop was held in the same crèche about a month later. It was marred by the invasion of the crèche by a group of older youths who insisted on using the place even though they had made no prior arrangements. It was only at the insistence of a research assistant who confronted the chairman of the local Civic

Association that the children were allowed to continue using the crèche. The outcome of this workshop was a set of beautiful clay masks moulded on the faces of the participating children. These were colourfully painted once they had set.

This was to be the first of many attempts by the project's research assistants to promote creative expression by the young people of New Crossroads. But it was an uphill struggle. The sheer battle for survival took centre stage more often than not.

Funding for the construction of the building was obtained from the Independent Development Trust, which had been set up by the last apartheid government in 1990 in a belated attempt to win the hearts and minds of black South Africans. I was one of the founding trustees. I let my name go forward in response to a request by the then leadership of the ANC in jail who urged me to help steer the IDT into pursuing progressive developmental strategies. The focus of the IDT's intervention was empowering the poorest of the poor through involvement in housing, education, health care, and rural development. The track record of the IDT between 1990-1997 showed not only how well the initial R2 billion was invested to yield an additional billion rand, but also that the IDT created valuable models for development among poor people across the country.

I felt that it was appropriate that the IDT should fund the capital costs of this Youth Centre. Young black poor children and youth represented the poorest of the poor. But even more importantly they represented the future and were already the largest proportion of the population and set to grow.

In the end the IDT contributed about R1 million. Running costs for the first three years were secured from the Rockefeller Brothers Fund and other donors such as Anglo & De Beer's Chairman's Fund, the Genesis Foundation, and Citizen Corporation of Boston made significant contributions. The community agreed that each household should contribute a set amount to be negotiated by the Civic Association. The University of Cape Town made contributions in kind. The latter took the form of time spent by myself and other colleagues who brought their expertise to planning, purchasing and providing the administrative infrastructure to manage the implementation of the project. Receipt and management of the funds for both capital and operational costs was a major part of the support given.

Establishing a management committee for the Youth Centre by the community was particularly problematic. Those with the requisite skills did not want to get involved. They cited unpleasant experiences with community initiatives as a reason. Consequently those who were elected onto the management committee were the willing horses, but not necessarily the most able. Eighteen people were elected, half of whom were young people to ensure that their views were taken into account in the planning and implementation of the Centre. The committee then elected an executive committee of five people to work alongside the management staff to ensure proper running of the facility.

The participation of the management committee in the planning and implementation process was limited by various factors: its lack of skills was considerable and although the chairperson was a woman of considerable energy, she had no experience in chairing a committee meeting, let alone in the management of a facility such as a youth centre. The other four members of the committee were elderly people with no organisational capacity. In addition, there was widespread apathy and lack of trust within the community which contributed to a lack of accountability by both the management committee and the staff.

There was also general cynicism towards any communal venture by residents who argued that they had been betrayed too often. They cited the abuse of money collected for community purposes such as the legal costs incurred during the battles against forced removals in the 1970s and 1980s. Most of the money collected then remains unaccounted for. There was a lack of trust in local leaders who were seen as feathering their own nests. This cynicism led to apathy and left the way open for the chair of the local Civic Association to dominate the decision-making process within New Crossroads – a perfect recipe for a self-fulfilling prophecy. Good citizens opted out of most communal activities in protest against corrupt practices, leaving those benefiting from corruption to have a field day.

It was against this background that a community meeting was held to discuss the contributions per household. An amount of R5 was suggested. Full participation would have raised a total of R8 000. There was a divergence of views on the appropriateness of household contributions. Earlier agreements in principle were challenged and fresh debate ensued. These excerpts are from the minutes:

'I've made my contribution of R5 so that future generations can see that their forefathers were working for a better future.'

'Why does Mamphela not go back to the donors and ask for more money?'

'People of New Crossroads, I have nothing in my pocket. There is nothing to eat at home. I am not working. Am I to be killed for not having R5 and be pointed out in the street that I did not pay the money and my house be set on fire? Remember in 1985 there was bloodshed because of money. People were killed. Is that what you are going to do to me?'

Concern about the corrupting influence of money and resultant killings was a recurring theme. People talked about their experiences in 1985 when their contributions disappeared and leaders weren't accountable. Blood did flow in the process of trying to sort out the problems. It became clear that cash contributions would not be forthcoming from residents.

Someone then suggested that the community consider contributions in kind in the form of building material. That too was rejected because people pleaded poverty arguing that buying building material would be far more expensive than the suggested R5 cash contribution per household. In the end the community promised to discuss the matter further and come back with a considered response.

I nonetheless pressed on with plans to build the Youth Centre, hoping that success would breed success. I felt that the deep-seated poor self-esteem the community had of itself could only be dispelled through patient confidence building. I hoped that getting the project going would show the community that we had confidence in them as partners. We also believed that turning the plans into concrete in both the metaphoric and physical sense would help dispel the fear that ours were the same empty promises that they had been fed before by government and other agencies. It was to be a long road from the ideal to reality.

In fact, where would the Centre have been had not the head of the University of Cape Town's Planning Department, Julian Elliot, intervened at a decisive moment to turn the dreams of the young people of New Crossroads into an affordable, aesthetically pleasing architectural plan? Thanks to him architectural drawings were produced which showed a structure comprised of a large central multipurpose hall, three seminar rooms, a lounge/dining area with a kitchenette, a library, a small computer room, an administrative office/reception area, and a caretaker's bachelor flat with a kitchenette and ablution facilities.

Construction started in March 1994 and was completed that October. The plot was fenced off and a low-maintenance garden with a large lawn and evergreen shrubs planted around the perimeter.

The appointment of staff was a challenge. Demands for local talent to be given an opportunity to run the Centre were huge. Advertisements for the directorship drew sixty applicants, most of whom were totally unsuitable for the job. They had not bothered to match their skills with the job description and requirements which had been clearly set out. There was an expectation by many of the applicants that they would be offered jobs available at the Centre simply because they were New Crossroads residents. An explosive mixture of desperation from years of unemployment and anger from having been denied educational opportunities lay behind most of the applications.

The only suitable applicant was a thirty-year-old white man called Alister Butler, who had spent time in the USA working in youth programmes. He both understood what was required and had innovative approaches to the challenges facing the youth of New Crossroads. There was a titanic struggle to get the management committee to accept the recommendation of the selection committee to appoint Butler director and offer the second-best candidate, Nobom Sonto, the deputy directorship. The recommendation was aimed at providing appropriate leadership drawing on the best local talent had to offer, as well as utilising the considerable expertise of someone from the wider society. We pointed out that in the nature of such development projects, Alister Butler would want to move on after two to three years, thus providing an opportunity for a smooth transition for well-trained local talent to take over the leadership position. The management committee grudgingly accepted the recommendation.

Other positions on offer were less contentious and went to local people of varying degrees of competence. The caretaker was a former Umkhonto weSizwe local commander, Mr Danisile, an able man dedicated to his community and reliable. The librarian, Mr Afrika, was somewhat out of his depth, but did his best to set up the library from scratch. He was later replaced by a University of the Western Cape graduate who was more suitable. The receptionist turned out to have been dishonest about her level of competence. She was shielded by the management committee from demonstrating her abilities in the essential skills before being appointed. The director acquiesced in a vain attempt to buy peace. He then had to spend a time training someone who had paper qualifications as a computer-literate secretary but who turned out to have inadequate secretarial training in the most elemental skills. She could hardly answer the phone, or use a computer, let alone do basic office tasks.

The price of peace was to be higher than the director had bargained for. The management committee set out in the first few months to make life difficult for him by challenging his decisions at every level. The chairperson insisted on micro-management by the committee. They were determined to show Butler that they held the key to his success. In their view white people had no leadership role in New Crossroads and they were determined to prove it.

Eventually the IDT facilitation unit had to be called in to help ease tensions between the management committee and the director. After many meetings it was conceded by the management committee that the director had been successful in mobilising local and other resources to mount an impressive youth programme which was popular with the young people. They were confronted with the dire consequences of their gate-keeping that was putting young people at further risk. The director in turn was made more sensitive to the complexities of empowering people whose instincts were to fear white domination in any black/white relationship given the legacy of the past.

One of the most complex post-apartheid issues is how to get black people to have enough self-confidence to acknowledge the damage of apartheid's social policies on their skills development. It takes a lot of self-confidence in a racist society to acknowledge ignorance without running the risk of that ignorance being equated with low intelligence. Racist prejudice has left too many black people with a sense of vulnerability at being stereotyped stupid when compared with white people. This burden is particularly onerous on young blacks with few positive black role models in their midst. It will take a major effort by both black and white South Africans to overcome the racist prejudices they have grown up with and work together to increase the skills' base so sorely needed for successful transition to a mature prosperous democracy. Too many white people are unconscious of the pain their attitudes of superiority cause black people. Too few acknowledge that the privileged educational status they enjoy and the benefits derived from it were made possible by the denial of opportunities to their black compatriots.

The challenge of social transformation in South Africa lies in bridging the chasm between legitimate black aspirations for a better future and the empowerment process that needs to be undertaken at all levels to enable poor people to participate meaningfully in forging a better future. White people's fears of being excluded from the benefits of citizenship also need to be addressed. The investment that the country has made in training the white population has to be husbanded. Developing a careful process of drawing on the talents of all those with skills to broaden the base of skills in a manner that makes white people believe that they have a stake in the success of this transformation process is essential. The practical application of such a process is however very demanding and risky as our experience in this project showed.

IV

The Centre was envisaged to play two complementary roles. It was to act as a vital information node enhancing access to information about services available to young people in the wider Cape Town area; and to be a place where some appropriate and affordable services would be rendered. The approach was driven by the view that an important aspect of poverty and deprivation is lack of access to information about even those meagre services that are available. There is also ignorance of the entitlements they have as citizens, despite the impressive efforts to popularise the South African Constitution and the basic rights of citizens it espouses.

The Centre positioned itself as an information node in a metropolitan network of services and programmes aimed at enriching the lives of young people. The provision of services on-site was tailored to get the best out of the limited resources available. There was also recognition of the need to provide space to bring in intellectual resources to augment the limited human resources of this township.

Alister Butler started as director in October 1994 and wasted no time in getting programmes going. He drew up a list of potential service providers from around the Cape Peninsula. A planning meeting was held at the Centre drawing eighty people from fifty NGO's. From this came a number of programmes focussing on adolescent sexuality, life skills and leadership development, sports and recreation, environmental awareness and education, cultural and creative arts, academic skills and support, income generation and unemployment issues.

Some of the ideas took off immediately and helped recruit young people to participate in the evolution of the programmes. Programmes with a focus on physical activity tended to be more popular than those requiring mental exertion.

Part of the life-skills programme included psychological counselling as child abuse was (and is) prevalent in this brutalised community. At the wider political level children are subject to structural violence. At the local community level they experience interpersonal abuse in the home, the street and the school environment. Counselling services for young people were sorely needed. The Trauma Centre was approached to assist as it provided counselling services for ex-political prisoners and detainees and had a good track record. It was also fortuitous that the director of the Trauma Centre was a psychologist who had assisted with individual psychological assessment and counselling of some of the adolescents at the Child Guidance Clinic based at the University of Cape Town. There was an opportunity for continuity of care. We arranged for a counsellor from the Trauma

Centre to run two group sessions per week for the young people and to provide individual counselling on occasion if this was required by the children.

Youth 2000, a leadership programme designed for troubled youth, became a partner with the Youth Centre to assist in other life-skills issues. This programme ran over a six-week period and assisted young people in improving their self-image and in setting realistic goals for themselves. The programme was also designed to initiate processes of self-reflection and to develop skills in conflict resolution.

The Quaker Peace Centre also brought in expertise in the field of conflict resolution, mediation, and peace work and ran two workshops at the Centre.

The Education Resource and Information Project, a local NGO affiliated to the University of the Western Cape, offered assistance with leadership training programmes. The focus of the courses was on problem solution, critical thinking, self-reflection and other essential leadership skills. There was also space for discussions on democracy, race and gender issues and their impact on the everyday lives of ordinary people.

The project's research showed that parents in New Crossroads generally avoided discussions about sex and sexuality with their children. This topic was taboo. It seemed that talking about sex was tantamount to engaging in the sexual act itself. How could one talk about sex to one's children without transgressing the incest taboo?

There were also many contradictory messages young people received from adults with respect to sex and sexuality. Sex was dirty. It was not to be contemplated as a normal physiological reality. Dignified people were not meant to be associated with sexual activity. Given the limited accommodation available to most households, many parents were forced to engage in sexual intercourse without adequate privacy. Children often had to pretend to be asleep while their parents were passionately engaged. There was a conspiracy of silence between parents and their children around the contradiction of engagement in 'sex' – as witnessed by their offspring – and continuing to label it as 'dirty'.

There was also a deep-seated resistance to all forms of contraception by young people. Contraception is seen as a licence for young people to have sex. In some households young girls who become pregnant were regarded as cheap, and punished through verbal and, in extreme cases, physical abuse. Even in the most well-meaning households, the use of contraceptives is viewed with suspicion. How does one know that one's daughter won't be sterile at the end of it all? Again, lack of information about how the human body is structured and functions, acts as a barrier to the utilisation of existing services.

These attitudes have particularly serious implications in an environment in which the spread of HIV/Aids has reached such alarming levels. Especially as the age group with the largest increase in HIV prevalence comprises fifteen- to twenty-five-year-old women. In fact young people are caught in the eye of a major storm. HIV/Aids is an epidemic of frightening proportions and the country is not in a good position to confront this massive challenge. Poor levels of education among those most vulnerable are hampering health-education drives. As pointed out earlier, the lack of an established science culture makes the understanding of cause and effect difficult to explain to most people. How do you describe the complexities of this epidemic to people with little understanding of how their bodies work? How do you transcend myths that accord causation to the realm of the supernatural and are thus not amenable to human intervention?

It is not surprising that President Thabo Mbeki also fell victim to dissident myths popularised on the Internet. The time wasted by the debate he raised over a period of eighteen months fuelled the fire of this pandemic. The delay in developing and implementing appropriate policies to curb the pandemic has cost the country heavily in lost productive lives.

South Africa is fortunate to have the scientific human capital, health infrastructure and financial resources to mount a comprehensive HIV/Aids programme. Brazil has done it off a slightly smaller base. What wants is political will. Technocratic debates should not stand in the way of sound policy interventions on the basis of what we know now.

The reticence in talking about sex further complicates matters. South Africa has yet to demonstrate its capacity to confront this challenge head-on. Breaking the silence around sex and sexuality is critical to the prevention and containment of this scourge.

135

In this regard we worked in partnership with the Planned Parenthood Association, an NGO with an excellent track record in developing training programmes on sexuality for young people. They were keen and identified a trained educator/nurse to implement their training programme and to provide on-site services as requested by the youth, free of charge. The educator ran workshops for both boys and girls at the Centre and provided contraceptive services. She also enlisted the support of the schoolteachers by visiting local schools and encouraging them to speak openly about sexuality or else invited experts to talk about these issues. There were some takers, but not as many as I'd hoped.

Parental support was canvassed through the management committee. Although many of them still felt reticent about discussions on sexuality, they were not hostile to the PPA's interventions. They understood that avoiding the issue did not make it go away and were more comfortable with someone else talking to their children about such issues. They made it clear that they were not like white people who talked about any- and everything to their children. They believed that parents would lose the respect of their children if they engaged in such talk.

The PPA educator encountered numerous problems, most notably that few utilised her service. Although she had approached schools to publicise the service, this had no real impact. She was forced to take a longer-term view in changing attitudes to contraception and helping young people take control over their own bodies. And some parents continued to be suspicious of the activities of the PPA because it was seen as breaking a taboo.

Other groups ran workshops at the Centre during the first year, complementing the work of the Planned Parenthood Association. These included Zikhulule Aids Project, ATTIC – the Aids Training, Information and Counselling Centre, Sexual Harassment Prevention and Support Services (SHARPSS) Aids programme through UCT's Students Health and Welfare Centres Organisation (SHAWCO), and the Triangle Health Care Project. The management committee of the Centre and parents in the community expressed hostility to education about homosexuality and gay rights. Some of these programmes had to be suspended.

During this time the director came under increasing attack by some members of the community. They accused him of promoting homosexuality at the Centre. All sorts of innuendo were spread about his sexual orientation and his close friendship with some of the boys at the Centre. At the heart of these attacks were two issues: the refusal to acknowledge homosexuality as a reality and discomfort with a white South African leading a project in a black township.

Many people in New Crossroads believed in the myth that homosexuality was alien to African culture. There was denial of even the possibility that the invisibility of homosexuality prior to 1994 had more to do with its repression than its non-existence. This denial was not limited to poor black South Africans but was reflected across socioeconomic classes, and indeed across the African continent. Witness the utterances of African leaders such as President Robert Mugabe of Zimbabwe in spite of a former colleague, Canaan Banana, being convicted in the Zimbabwean High Court of rape and sexual abuse of male security personnel. President Museweni of Uganda is equally adamant that there is no place in Uganda for homosexuality. South Africa is the only country in Africa to enshrine the protection against discrimination on the basis of sexual orientation in its Constitution. But social practice remains mired in traditional notions of acceptable sexual behaviour. Alister Butler became a scapegoat for this community's inability to confront the reality of different sexual orientations. He was seen as 'teaching' young people to be gay rather than recognising that he was merely opening space for discussion of the issue as part of a deeper understanding of sexuality.

The issue of discomfort with a white person leading a project in a black township was understandable though counterproductive in the long term. The reality of the legacy of apartheid is that there are few black people in the townships who have the requisite skills and experience to successfully run projects. In this case the search for the directorship had demonstrated that there were just no local skills to undertake this task. But the need for redress of past discrimination, the need to be seen to be in control of their own destiny, and the lack of insight into the complexity of running a project like this led to the view that they did not need a white person's leadership. The fact that he was gay made him even more illegitimate in their view. As elsewhere, the failure to creatively manage the tension between the skills' gaps in the black community and their impatience with skills development, has led to the appointment of black people beyond their level of competence in many areas. This unfortunately further feeds the myth of inherent black incompetence.

It was tragic to see how prejudice could undermine an exciting project. In the end I advised Butler to stand down and leave the Centre for his own safety. We reached an amicable settlement, and the deputy director, Sonto, took over the position. She struggled to rise to the challenge. Her innate intelligence was not adequate compensation for the management expertise required nor had she any experience in dealing with the people in such a setting.

Then a series of rapes occurred across the road from the Centre. In one case, a girl who frequented the Centre was raped. This emphasised the importance of developing programmes to examine issues of gender and sexual violence. Such programmes had to involve both boys and girls, yet it was clear that separate workshops would be necessary in some instances. It was suggested that the services of an organisation such as Ilitha Labantu which deals directly with abuse and rape in Guguletu should be secured.

Ilitha Labantu was a project started by a woman who was a survivor of an abusive marriage. Once she walked out of her marriage she begun taking in victims of abusive relationships to give them a break and a chance to make more rational decisions about their own futures. Ilitha had grown into a regional programme with its own premises. It worked as a facilitator to help community groups including religious communities to acknowledge and confront abusive relationships. Consequently, it had the potential to play an invaluable role in running workshops at the Centre. But the new director wasn't keen on the idea. It seemed that lack of self-confidence and petty jealousies played a role in preventing this programme from going ahead.

Another of the programmes initiated by the Centre tackled the nonexistence of sports facilities. In neighbouring Guguletu there was a soccer field, and karate lessons were offered. The need for sports facilities in New Crossroads itself was clear. The research team suggested that we run indoor sports training at the Centre in karate, basketball, netball, and table tennis. It was also suggested that we hire professional instructors to teach children these sports. We also enlisted the support of the Civic Association to develop adjoining land into a playing field.

The Centre initiated a number of important sporting activities. Basketball became not only the most popular, but also the most successful from a competitive point of view. Sportsman's Warehouse sponsored the team with outfits and balls. The availability of basketball hoops within the Centre helped make it a success.

Rondebosch Boys School also offered fencing lessons to a group of boys from the Centre. In fact the Cape Town Youth Fencing Championships held their 1995 competition at the Youth Centre. This made history. Not only was it the first time such a competition was held at a township venue, but one of the young people of New Crossroads won the Sportsmanship Cup.

In other codes such as athletics, boxing, netball, and soccer much progress was made in engaging young people in active sports. One could feel the hum of activity at the Centre. Young people acquired a shine in their eyes – they at last had something to look forward to in life. Extramural activities provided new meaning and hope. Sadly, but not surprisingly, participation by girls lagged behind that of boys, because the girls were often burdened with domestic chores, leaving them little time for recreation. The risks of attacks, both sexual and physical, also made those who were free to come hesitant to walk to the Centre unless accompanied by someone who could protect them.

SCORE, an international sports development programme run by USA college students, also came to lend a hand. They held three workshops covering soccer, basketball and athletics.

The Wilderness Leadership School and Earth Life Africa played a critical role in promoting environmental awareness programmes at the Centre and in New Crossroads as a whole. The children were given the opportunity to take part in campaigns to better the environment in the township itself by initiating cleaning parties as well as putting pressure on local authorities to provide better services. Opportunities for linking up with organisations promoting tree-planting were also explored to secure donations of trees and to provide incentives for covering the harsh Cape sand with new life.

The response of all the groups we approached was overwhelmingly positive. Young people were excited about being part of something new that could transform the landscape of their township. They linked up with similar groups from Langa, Nyanga and Mitchell's Plain, and were generally the most organised group operating out of the Centre. They divided their activities into sections, each headed by a leader. Bulelwa was the leading light here. They organised three hiking trails with the help of the Wilderness Leadership School, arranged a beach hike from Strandfontein to Kogelbaai, and went on a tour hosted by the National Botanical Society. A whole new world was opened for these young people away from the crime, grime and deprivation of their environment.

An interesting approach adopted by this group was the establishment of ground rules about interpersonal relationships. Boys and girls were treated as equals. No sexism was tolerated. Offenders were reprimanded by their peers and made to mend their ways. Love affairs within the group were also discouraged in the interest of the broader purpose of group cohesion. The focus was on learning more about their environment without the tensions that usually accompany teenage love relationships. This was an innovative way of managing the group.

The group also developed a candle-making enterprise to raise money for their activities. They held a candlelight dinner at the Centre to which their parents were invited. The dinner served to raise both money and awareness of the group and its activities. It was a success on both counts. Children at the Centre made candles for each table. They also served food to the guests. A local band played and talented young singers were able to showcase their performance skills. The hosts for the evening were a young man and woman from the environmental group.

This group's success was demonstrated in many ways including taking part in Arbour Day celebrations and securing donations of trees from the Trees for Africa Project which were planted in churchyards, the local home for the disabled, the Youth Centre and other public spaces. They also linked up with City Council workers to promote regular refuse removal, spearheading several clean-up campaigns.

Another of the Centre's aims was to channel youthful energy into creative directions. The great need for self-expression among young people in such deprived environments shows up in many forms. The graffiti culture around the world attests to this need. New Crossroads is no exception. On entering the township your are greeted by angry, amusing and sometimes clever graffiti. In the apartheid era the focus was on bravado. Defying the ban on ANC and PAC activities in the pre-1990 period took the form of proclaiming support for these banned organisations by repeating their slogans in bright colours on the walls of public buildings: 'One settler one bullet!' 'The people shall govern!' 'Down with apartheid!'

We secured the support of many knowledgeable people within and outside the community to promote creativity among young people. Success was uneven in the areas of painting, jazz, dance, storytelling, drama, and these efforts were difficult to sustain given the demands on volunteers and the limitation of organisational skill and leadership at the directorship level.

Facilities for a library were part of the original plan of the Youth Centre. The librarian had his work cut out stocking the library to cover the age group six to twenty years, guiding children to use appropriate reading matter for school projects as well as encouraging a culture of reading for pleasure. Prior to this library the children of New Crossroads had very little access to books which were always in short supply at school and most families had no books in their homes. The library adopted a policy of not lending books for home use to ensure the broadest possible access to the limited stock and to reduce losses. READ, a national NGO promoting reading in poor communities, helped to compile a book list for the library so that the budget could be spent to its greatest advantage.

The librarian developed a programme for the library group. Bulelwa again demonstrated her leadership qualities by volunteering to assist in the library to catalogue books, show children how the library worked and acting as a storyteller to younger children twice a week. The library group launched the library in partnership with the environmental group and tried to make the community at large aware of the importance of the library – a tall order in a community with such low literacy levels.

Very few people in New Crossroads read for pleasure. Attempts to incorporate reading in all activities in the Centre were only partially successful. Children not used to being read to had difficulties retaining an interest and it took enormous energy and skill to hold their attention long enough for them to start enjoying handling the books and following the stories. Bulelwa was alone in persisting with this activity, but sustaining it over the long term became difficult without a greater commitment from the staff at the Centre. Attempts to form reading groups in the older age groups did not yield much success either. Physical activities were far more attractive than reading which was associated with painful school experiences and perceptions of failure. Physical prowess gave instantaneous satisfaction and a sense of mastery.

The damage done to the culture of people living on the edge of survival goes beyond material deprivation. Indigenous African cultures had their own richness. The paucity of literacy did not necessarily imply intellectual poverty. Nor did the oral culture lack in richness of language. Storytelling was a powerful tool to promote the communication of the richness of language, the core values of each community, and to showcase the prowess of the storyteller in dipping into the proverbs, metaphors and figures of speech that reflected the wealth of knowledge embedded in each language. Storytelling also provided a bridge between generations and a relaxed forum around the family hearth for the older generation to pass on the wisdom inherited from their elders while also providing entertainment for the young.

I had the good fortune of growing up in a household where my father's maternal grandmother fulfilled the role of the storyteller. She was already in her late eighties when I started school in 1954. But she was an active woman whose intelligence was not masked by her illiteracy. She walked stooped on her walking stick but did a number of chores sitting down with her legs folded beneath her – quite a feat attesting to her agility in her younger days. She rocked babies to sleep, she peeled vegetables, washed up and still continued to make lovely reed mats with interesting patterns made from a variety of coloured string she used to bind the reeds together.

Storytelling preceded bedtime over weekends. During the week we had school homework to do. Washing up after supper was a chore easily borne as a prelude to the entertainment awaiting us around my mother's black coal stove – a shining Welcome Dover. My great grandmother loved seeing my siblings and I jostle to sit as close to her as possible. The youngest always got the prime position. We all sat on floor mats made from softened leather or reeds from the near-by river. We not only enjoyed listening to the stories but also watching her watery eyes light up with excitement as she emphasised a point. The closer you sat, the more you could also pick up the nuances of the story as she rocked from side to side to make a point or to simulate movement. Sometimes her walking stick came in handy to illustrate the lie of a particular object in relation to others.

My knowledge of Northern Sesotho, my mother tongue, was considerably enriched by these encounters. She also taught us riddles and got us to compete in finding solutions to them. Even though we grew up in an area with a different dialect from my parents' we did not have problems in keeping our spoken and written language pure. We also had the advantage of listening to the many proverbs carrying the core values of our culture. The wisdom embedded in some of the mystical stories shaped my development in a significant way.

I still remember the story that resembled the myth of Sisyphus. It was about a woman whose daughter was trapped in an abusive marriage. The custom in that ethnic group under the rule of King Moloto was that no woman could divorce her husband unless she could prove that she was strong enough to roll a large boulder up the little hill near the King's court. The boulder was known as Ramanyobatsoko-tlane (the victor over the mighty). The mother of the abused woman offered to roll the rock up to secure her daughter's freedom. There was widespread scepticism about her ability to accomplish what even men could not. Many who had tried could not overcome the combined challenge of the weight of the mighty boulder and the force of gravity. The boulder always ended up the victor as it rolled back to its stubborn position at the base of the hill. This woman surprised everybody by tying her skirts into a formation like a pair of pants, and then bending down to slowly make her way up the hill with her precious cargo. She did not look back but kept going inch by inch. The most delicate of manoeuvres came when she reached the precarious summit where many had witnessed their efforts undone by the force of gravity pulling down the heavy boulder. She was not to be defeated. She hung in there for dear life and became the first and last woman to meet this challenge. She gave a new meaning to the proverb in Sesotho: *Mmage ngoana otshwara thipa ka bogaleng* –

only a mother of a child can grab the sharp end of a knife in protection of her child.

It is a cruel irony that the young people of New Crossroads and other townships are denied the opportunities to develop their language competence as well as their personalities through the rich cross-pollination that can be drawn on between generations. The process of urbanisation coupled with the lack of modern facilities and grinding poverty has left them without the support they are entitled to from adults. The results are tragic: poor language development, inability to communicate, poor self-image, aggressive behaviour that remains the only channel for venting frustration.

The success of child-to-child programmes as well as peer counselling has been widely demonstrated across cultures and national boundaries. I drew on these experiences to design a mentoring programme that involved university students resident in New Crossroads assisting younger people with their studies at the Centre. There was little enthusiasm from these students. Many of them were struggling with their own studies under difficult conditions and could not make time to take responsibility for younger people. The Youth Centre did not have the resources to offer financial inducements so we had to abandon this aspect of the programme.

Attempts to get local teachers in a programme of learning and questioning outside the classroom were also unsuccessful. As many teachers end their school day exhausted from handling large classes with inadequate resources or suffer from poor motivation, there is little energy for extramural activities. The few who were interested were already overextended in trying to cope with multiple responsibilities in a poorly resourced setting.

A major success, however, was the hosting of a Winter School during the mid-year holidays. The programme included input from Education Alive, a local NGO. Personnel from this group helped older high school students with study techniques at the Centre. The students also had the opportunity of discussing what prevented them from studying in their home environments. Among the problems were: drug abuse by members of their households, peer pressure to socialise instead of studying, lack of encouragement from parents and pressure for young people to do household tasks instead of schoolwork, let alone crowded and noisy conditions in the homes.

Grassroots Educare Trust worked with younger children in Grades 1-3. They ran sessions alerting the children to child abuse and to the risks of physical and sexual abuse. Using waste material they showed the children how to make educational toys, organised rhythm, dance and storytelling activities and took the children on a visit to a local farm – all with great success.

Because computer literacy was of prime interest to many young people, the Centre was hoping to set up a computer room with someone to run the programme but lack of resources prevented this. Given the demands of the hi-tech information world we live in, young people in New Crossroads are at risk of further marginality. The digital divide takes on a real meaning in this community.

Children from all groups active at the Centre attended Aids Day activities in the city at the end of 1995, saw an exhibition at the National Art Gallery, and supported a march against child abuse. On June 16, National Youth Day, the Centre had young people painting murals on the wall across the street. These murals depicted and promoted the various activities at the Centre. Paint was donated by the City Council of Cape Town, that also helped to clear the rubbish dump bordering the mural. I felt this was an important statement by the City Council in that it realised its responsibility for clean environments for all the children of the city, not just the privileged white few.

At about this time I read about the innovative work of Dr Joanne Tortorici from UNICEF who had worked with schoolteachers in Nicaragua in an attempt to encourage teachers to explore new ways of disciplining their pupils without corporal punishment. Her approach helped teachers deal with their own frustrations without resorting to physical violence. Violent responses in everyday situations were prevalent in Nicaragua due to the impact of civil war – a situation akin to our own. We used some of her ideas in running workshops for both parents and teachers to assist them in non-violent disciplinary methods.

In addition, the School of Education at the University of Cape Town was approached to provide a programme addressing non-violent disciplinary methods. It was clear to me that workshops were needed for both parents and teachers on a regular basis if we were to assist the adults and the children. Unfortunately, sustaining a programme of this nature proved too difficult in this community.

A critical missing factor was a champion who could inspire confidence within the community and be open to outside help and ideas. Attempts to draw parents into taking a greater interest in the development of their own children included encouraging them to participate in the activities of the Youth Centre. We saw the promotion of communication between parents and children as essential to improving understanding and reducing the tensions between them. It would also have given parents a relaxed time to enjoy their children.

A successful parent meeting was held at the Centre towards the end of its first year and some seventy parents from New Crossroads came to hear us report back on the activities. We took the opportunity to stress the importance of their support for the Centre. During the Winter School students had complained that there were many barriers to studying at home. Often their parents did not appreciate the importance of study and homework, and poor communication between the generations worsened matters.

A member of the National Legislative Assembly who addressed the gathering focussed on the social problems in New Crossroads and suggested ways in which parents could assist in tackling some of these. Other speakers urged parents to take an interest in their children's developmental activities by, for instance, watching them compete in games and helping them with homework. Discussions included such issues as health, crime, the concept of ubuntu, and sex education, which drew all the negative responses with which we were already familiar.

Exhibition tables had been set up and the parents were encouraged to find out about their children's activities. Some were enthusiastic and offered to assist the Youth Centre by guarding against vandalism, making costumes for children and making donations of food for various functions. The spirit at the meeting was so positive that staff, children and parents were infected by the enthusiasm.

When the Centre was officially opened the following year it drew people from both the local township and its neighbours, as well as those from afar. In fact the opening coincided with the 1996 Local Authority election campaigns and brought political heavyweights such as Tokyo Sexwale, then Premier of Gauteng Province, and others to the ceremony. They might have used it as an election platform but the occasion was also a morale booster to this poor community that was seldom visited by dignitaries. Locals got an opportunity to see the people who claimed to represent them in Parliament at the national, regional and local levels. They could feel connected to the corridors of power, although many were too wise to be lulled into a false sense of importance by this kind of visit. They knew enough of politicians not to expect much from electioneering encounters.

Nevertheless it was a day of celebration with music, food and friendship. The youth could show off their talents and accomplishments, and the director left satisfied with a job well done.

IV

In retrospect I feel the New Crossroads Youth Centre succeeded in a number of important ways. It showed the community what could be achieved through pooling resources from both the locals and those well-disposed people in the wider society. It also demonstrated how much creativity was waiting to be unleashed from both the young and old of New Crossroads, as the Centre became a hub of activity.

Much was achieved over the first eight months period of peak activity. Operational administrative structures were set up and roles were clarified between the staff and management committee. Clear job descriptions were formalised. The Centre worked successfully with NGOs who in the majority of cases rendered their services free of charge. The director nurtured a variety of youth groups into becoming active participants and many of the youth's activities were self-motivated, drawing on knowledge of local creativity and organisational skills honed through political and church experience. Local volunteers were incorporated into the Centre's activities by assisting the youth in workshops and with their activities.

The Centre attracted the interest of many government officials and ministers who participated in its various functions. A number of them promised to give the Centre tangible support, but like most political promises this did not, in the end, materialise. Effective use was made of the media, of television and of Radio Xhosa to help advertise and popularise activities at the Centre which was seen as a beacon of hope.

There were striking failures. The most important one being the constraints imposed by a weak human and intellectual resource base. People who have little education, who have been betrayed often and who have a poor self-image are difficult to mobilise for creative action. As I've pointed out, 'learned helplessness' is real, as is a lack of basic trust. Then again, once community participation is mobilised, sustaining it becomes an intense and demanding activity. I underestimated what this would entail.

I was repeatedly shocked by the ease with which members of the community tolerated 'untruthfulness'. During the struggle against apartheid truthfulness could in many cases have led to the betrayal of one's comrades with dire consequences. Yet in our context where social transformation was the goal, turning a blind eye or defending comrades who might be involved in wrongdoing was self-defeating, and the Centre did not escape these attitudes.

Allegations of misuse and abuse of power were many and frequent. For instance, the second director began to use the resources and facilities for her own private benefit. It was rumoured that the vehicle donated by Caltex to the Centre was used by her brother to run a taxi service. Computers at the Centre were carefully guarded for use by the director and her favoured few. The Internet facility was not made available to other members of staff. Bulelani complained that one of his friends had been denied access to a computer to draw up his CV so he could apply for jobs. The list of complaints was endless.

By the end of the second year activity levels at the Centre had dropped dramatically. A few activities remained such as basketball, a choir, and gumboot dancing, but these had become sporadic and disorganised. Many of the young people in my project stopped using the Centre because they were afraid to venture into the area, afraid of the gang activity. Two years later the Centre had run out of steam. There were sad scenes of recriminations and finger-pointing, but little energy to intervene creatively.

The director also found greener pastures and was no longer interested in continuing to work with that community. My own responsibilities as Vice Chancellor of the University of Cape Town with its own transformation pressures left little time for me to actively intervene. My attempts to call meetings of the management committee were frustrated by poor attendance. In the end I had to accept that, without the inner resources to sustain development, poor communities such as New Crossroads were unlikely to cope with the demands of running modern institutions. It would take a full-time champion to nurture sustainable development in such a community.

My hope that the local authorities would intervene to provide support was dashed by their own lack of ability to govern. The same factors that hamper the development of poor communities, plagues government at the local, provincial and national levels. When I read that the national government only managed to spend one per cent of its welfare budget for poverty relief, I weep for the new South Africa. Similarly I was left grieving at the lost opportunities of the national Ministry of Health's inability to spend forty per cent of its Aids budget in the midst of the crying need to support victims of the world's most frightening pandemic. At the heart of the failure of government departments to deliver is their unwillingness to utilise expertise where it exists outside the ANC. This reluctance is understandable in the quest to prove that the ANC is capable of governance, but it is an expensive option in the face of continuing racism and a lack of confidence in a majority black government. Failures are expensive for poor people and do nothing to reduce the prejudice of white racists. If anything such failures are used as proof of inherent black incompetence.

Opportunities for development in the City of Cape Town which has the requisite expertise to adequately manage the resources of the city equitably, continue to follow the contours set by the legacy of racial discrimination and geographic marginalisation of poor black people. Those able to escape into suburban environments get to enjoy the prosperity of the Mother City. Young people of New Crossroads, like many around South Africa who are trapped in dysfunctional urban locations, continue to be let down by adults. It was a sad day when the Youth Centre closed its doors.

CHAPTER EIGHT

The challenge
Dealing with the legacy

I

I believe one of the major aspects highlighted by this project was that despite the failure of society to nurture young people, some of them still succeed in developing into healthy functional adults. The cost of both success and failure is high. But then the legacy of apartheid will remain a millstone around the collective and individual necks of poor people unless creative social policies are enacted, implemented and monitored. A lot more thought needs to be given to strengthening poor communities to promote trust within them and to allow the building of institutions and institutional relationships. Undoing the legacy of the past will take a lot of courage, time, energy and patience.

II

For me, the triumph of the human spirit was best captured in the narratives of Bulelwa and Bulelani.

Bulelwa was a woman with a mission who refused to be kept down by racism, sexism, poor social services, a deserting father, and a mother who periodically collapsed emotionally under the sheer weight of the challenges facing her as a single parent with no means of support. Even more remarkable was Bulelwa's ability to confront and satisfactorily resolve the moral dilemmas posed by the demands of the collective that undermined personal development.

She succeeded largely because she had self-confidence and a sense of purpose larger than her personal life. Her charm and integrity also won her friends and supporters who made a difference in her life. She was always available to give leadership and support to those less able to make it on their own. For example, she volunteered to read to younger children and to act as a storyteller at the Youth Centre library. She served on the Youth Centre Management Committee to ensure young people had representation. She acted as a trail guide for the Wilderness Leadership School to expose township youths to the beauty of the Cape Peninsula. All these activities enriched others and developed Bulelwa's leadership capabilities.

But Bulelwa was equally content to be unpopular if this meant the freedom to pursue her dreams. She fell back on friendships with her sisters to protect herself from the hostility of an envious neighbourhood. She realised that friendships with local peers would come at a high cost – to rebel against authority meant forming risky relationships that could lead to unwanted pregnancy or substance abuse.

Bulelwa's outgoing nature enabled her to feel at ease with people outside her environment. From these people she drew strength and inspiration which broadened her horizons. She was able to observe, discuss and experiment with different approaches to life's challenges beyond the constraints of New Crossroads. In short, she developed a rich reservoir of ways of being human that sustained her through the difficult patches in her life.

Bulelwa also took the initiative in seeking support. For example, when she completed her high-school education, she successfully approached the Italian Embassy to fund her correspondence course at Damelin College. This Further Commercial Education Diploma launched her on a career path in the commercial world. Her keen intellect and charming personality had made her entry and progression in the workplace relatively easy.

I celebrated with her when she got married in 1997 and again in 1999 when she proudly told me of the birth of her first child, a son. When I last saw her she and her husband lived in their own flat in a suburban Cape Town neighbourhood. Her mother was a proud grandmother who helped out with childcare. Gone were the days of anxiety about sheer survival. It was a joy to have her as one of my guests at the farewell function when I left the University of Cape Town in April 2000. She was relaxed and gorgeous as ever in her evening gown. She had successfully steered her way into adulthood.

III

Bulelani was equally remarkably successful. He defied death twice in serious motor vehicle accidents – triumphed over inadequate road safety provisions in poor neighbourhoods. He carved a path for himself above the violent culture consuming his neighbourhood. Yet he refrained from looking down upon his peers who were less successful, displaying a compassionate understanding of the enormity of the challenges they faced. In fact, he was painfully aware that had he not chosen to subject himself to parental discipline he would have come to nothing. This made him continually challenge his peers about slipping into the seemingly inevitable. He had not given up on them. He kept hoping that the community and society at large would wake up to their responsibilities of providing more creative and supportive environments for all young people.

Bulelani's passion for education as the path out of poverty and powerlessness was shared by his mother. She gave him consistent support in his development into young adulthood. His passion sometimes threatened to consume him when he drove himself too hard. He did not allow himself any failures. The limitations of his intellectual capacity – a residue of the two motor vehicle accidents and an outcome of poor-quality primary education – frustrated him to the point of engaging in self-destructive actions. Banging his head against a wall to force his brain to understand mathematics, was an example. He had little time for fun and games. For a young man raised in these circumstances to successfully complete a technikon diploma in engineering was a major achievement.

The path into adulthood was for him further complicated by being male in an environment in which few positive male models exist. Although his mother's brothers stood in for his deceased father and supported him during his traditional Xhosa initiation ritual, they played no meaningful role in actively guiding him during his childhood and youth. On the contrary, his mother had to leave the extended family home because she could not tolerate her brothers' uncouth behaviour. By his own admission Bulelani had no role models to rely on. He was astute enough to take the best he could out of traditional life without being imprisoned by it.

But he paid a heavy price. He lamented the loneliness he had to endure. He yearned for love and friendship, yet his attempts to get closer to people ended in failure. The moving love poem he wrote during his high school days reflected his pain. He was likely to continue into mature adulthood as a lonely man, because he did not identify with the popular notion of what it meant to be a man. Nor did he believe in violence or dominance of others because they were smaller, weaker or less important. He failed to find someone to teach him how to be a man without the negative associations with the male dominance of a patriarchal system. He realised that he would have to define manhood for himself. His was a difficult and lonely journey through youth.

IV

Both Bulelwa and Bulelani had a strong sense of self and definite purpose. Both demonstrated strong leadership and responsibility for their actions. They had a firm focus on the future and applied themselves diligently to their education in spite of the poor schooling they received in the early part of their development. They were both able to transcend the limited horizons of their environment without losing touch with it just as they successfully negotiated the limitations of their family support systems in times of crises.

There are countless examples of triumphs against the odds by children and young people around the world. But there are also and always casualties. The narratives of other members of the group showed a mixture of success and failure as they too steered by the stars into an uncertain future. Their personal resources were found wanting in many respects and they could not handle the pressures of their inadequate and unpredictable society. For example, Lolo, the shy young woman who had to endure poverty and an abusive father, lacked the self-confidence to explore life beyond the confines of her home and community.

V

What seems to characterise the legacy of apartheid on the vital institutions of society is the uncertainty that comes from rapid change in fortunes at the personal, family, school, and wider community level. In fact, uncertainty permeates every facet of the lives of the residents of New Crossroads. It has bred deep insecurity and mistrust.

Whereas the family is meant to provide a safe haven in life's troubled waters, in New Crossroads uncertainty permeates family life in a manner difficult for outsiders to comprehend. The family unit cannot be taken for granted and the availability of a mother, let alone both parents, is a luxury few children enjoy. In addition, the provision of basic needs is beyond the means of many, and trusting and respectful relationships are an exception rather than the rule. The family is under siege from the combined legacy of the migrant labour system, poverty, adherence to outmoded traditions, and the changing roles of men and women as gender politics is reconfigured everywhere in post-apartheid South Africa.

Young people in New Crossroads are separated from their parents due to a circular migration between the Eastern Cape Province and Cape Town, and because of an adherence to outmoded customs. In the first instance, since colonial times labour policies have separated families. Men were forced to live in appalling conditions as units of labour in overcrowded compounds in urban areas in order to support their families who were confined by law to rural areas. Their short visits home were inadequate to nurture an enduring sense of family. Consequently, young people grew up with little knowledge of their fathers as important figures in their lives. The dismantling of apartheid has not erased the patterns of behaviour entrenched by this system.

The inadequacy and uncertainties of township life for poor people forces many to hedge their bets between the urban and rural areas. Urban life offers access to job opportunities, while the village provides the security of tradition and the rituals with kin and kith. For many, 'home' remains the village homestead and they continue to idealise rural life and have dreams of retiring to its peace and quiet. Major rituals such as marriage and circumcision are conducted at the rural base, and the dead are still taken 'home' for burial in communal graveyards.

Being forced to run – and to run between – dual households puts an added strain on already limited resources. Usually one parent is forced to spend time servicing the 'home' thus depriving children of care. During the project I came across some cases of single parents leaving their offspring alone to fend for themselves for months in New Crossroads while they were fulfilling their rural obligations. Extended family members also make claims on city-based relatives to share whatever they have with them. Visits from rural relations put an additional strain on the limited resources – space, financial and emotional. Attempts by parents to protect their offspring from violence in the township also contribute to a discontinuity of care by parents and insecurity as children are shuttled between the urban and rural bases. Many of the young people in our project had to change schools three to four times while shuttling between the two poles.

Uncertainty in the family also comes from an adherence to outmoded customs. For example, by demanding that children born before marriage be left in the maternal home causes untold pain. There are numerous cases I came across of the negative consequences of this practice. It alienates children from the affectionate care of their mothers, in many instances from a very tender age. The sense of being abandoned by your mother is hardly a good foundation on which to build self-confidence. If your mother abandons you, what worth can you attach to yourself?

This custom puts women in the difficult position of choosing between marriage and their own offspring. It cannot be easy to simply walk away from the responsibility of nurturing your offspring in the name of custom. The anxiety and sense of guilt this induces has significant implications for the quality of life of affected women. It's worth asking: how do women bear the pain of making such an impossible choice?

Abandoning children in this way creates mistrust between adults and children. How can children trust adults who fail to disclose to them who their real biological parents and siblings are? It is not just the failure to disclose which is problematic. The discovery of the identity of your real mother, father and siblings later in life and through indirect sources adds to the sense of insecurity. For example, Lunga grew up in his maternal grandparents' home relishing the love of his 'uncle'. Nearly twenty years later this 'uncle' turned out to be Lunga's mother's first-born who had been left in her parent's care.

The discovery threw him into an identity crisis. What else did he not know about his origins and his real biological connections to those around him? How does he adjust to being a second-born with much reduced ritual status so late in his life? How does he continue to trust and respect the integrity of his parents under these circumstances?

The impact of this custom on relationships between adults and children is significant given the high proportion of affected children. A custom that may have made sense when the incidence of births out of wedlock was low, is inappropriate now. Consider Dumo who had a promising future until his mother abandoned him at the age of fourteen in favour of a husband who was promptly arrested and jailed for selling marijuana. Dumo's life was further shattered when he was abandoned for the second time by his mother's brother who was struggling under the weight of unreasonable demands by an extended family. Within two years the confident fourteen-year-old had dissolved into an uncertain and self-doubting adolescent. In the end Dumo failed to complete his high school education because his family, community and society failed him. The future of an uneducated young man like himself in a modern socioeconomic country in which skills are vital to income generation cannot be bright. In addition his self-esteem must have been dented by the realisation that his mother had chosen a man who turned out to be a jailbird over her own flesh and blood. Dumo's earlier philosophical response to the separation as an essential part of tradition has over the years given way to distress and despair as his fortunes declined. The last time I saw him he was a sad cynical twenty-two-year-old unskilled labourer.

In the group of sixteen young people only seven experienced a continuity of care by their mothers. Two others besides Dumo had been abandoned by their mothers. Pule was abandoned at birth and Lolo in early childhood. These two young women both have a poor self-image. The unspoken question on their minds was one I've already asked: if your mother doesn't care for you, are you worth anything at all? Both Lolo and Pule were like flower buds that have curled into themselves and failed to open up. They both responded warmly to human kindness and intimacy. Hugging them made me realise how such a simple gesture confirms another's humanity.

I also realised how much could be achieved by making opportunities available to young people like these to enable them to open up to life's possibilities. Often I felt powerless given the limitations of my own resources to respond in a sustainable way to them.

There seems to be little appreciation of the value of the emotional nurture of children by the majority of families in this community. A condition similar in many others struggling with poverty. The impact of the dramatic shift from tenderness – that extends from birth until the child is about two years old – to the harsh treatment of older children, is underestimated. Harshness towards older children is treated as part of the normal process of weaning children from the breast. The situation does not permit firmness to be tempered with gentleness towards the growing child.

The trauma of adjusting to this dramatic change in the quality of care from one's parents is the equivalent of moving from first- to third-class citizenship. Often this is further complicated by the physical absence of your parents and lack of space to express your pain in these circumstances.

My own childhood experiences as told in my autobiography, *Mampela Ramphele – A Life*, remain vivid in this regard. It was only through making myself useful as an assistant child minder that I managed to secure a close relationship with my mother as she turned her attention to my younger siblings. I made myself indispensable to her in order to secure my place alongside my younger siblings.

This lack of attention to the emotional needs of children is also reflected in the ease with which children are dispersed between relatives. Whatever concerns mothers may have about separation are often overruled by their in-laws, including the children's father. The notion that children belong to the patrilineage gives the father a greater say in these matters than the mother who is often the primary caregiver. Moving children between relatives is a common way of dealing with material scarcity. It is intended to spread the risk between several households and to establish and confirm obligations between extended family members as an insurance policy against unknown future risk. The dispersion of children also serves other extended family objectives such as the need for grandparents to have someone to run errands for them in their old age. Such children become caregivers to ailing and ageing grandparents with little attention to their own needs for love and care. The insecurity these practices breed needs to be taken into account in helping poor families cope with child rearing.

Watching one of my younger brothers subjected to the trauma of being taken to our paternal grandparents about sixty kilometres away against my mother's wishes, remains with me as a painful memory. He had to endure the harshness of physical separation from his parents, and the deprivation of the most basic material comforts our nuclear family was accustomed to. Worst of all, he was treated as a convenience by my father in discharging his responsibilities to his parents. None of my brother's emotional needs were attended to. It took years of support and encouragement by me to repair the damage to his self-esteem. He turned out to be a successful adult whose life was cut short by a cruel malignancy in his early forties.

Poverty adds to the burden of families. Desertion by fathers is often prompted by their inability to bear the burden of being primary providers. The burden of failure becomes intolerable for those who lack of the capacity to generate enough income as uneducated and unskilled labourers. Desertion is not always physical, it can also be emotional. Many men 'die' as parents and husbands by indulging in alcohol, drugs or becoming unresponsive to their families. Women end up carrying a disproportionate load of responsibility in the nurturing of young people without the necessary authority to do so. Lolo's mother, for instance, threw in the towel and set off to find a better life without the burdens of a dysfunctional family.

Bulelwa's mother exemplifies the burdens women have to carry when they're abandoned by their husbands. That Bulelwa's father and his family could deprive his children of material support, and be assisted by the police to do so, is a scandal that needs to be banished from post-apartheid South Africa. There is a need to support women in this position so that they can make the necessary claims to secure their children's rights. The Constitution with its focus on child protection and gender equity provides a basis for relief for women caught up in situations like these. But constitutional provisions have yet to find expression in the everyday lives of people in poor communities.

The sheer weight of poverty also renders families less able to support their children. Both Mthetheleli and Phalo are prime examples of how grinding poverty undermines family life in spite of both parents being present. Mthetheleli's physical and emotional abuse by his parents undermined his self-confidence and left him with poorly developed social skills, making it difficult for him to endear himself to others who could assist him. At a farewell get-together for the group, Mthetheleli greedily ate the snacks without regard to sharing with others and afterwards left the visitor's toilet in such a mess that no one else could use it.

I was pleasantly surprised to learn from a recent follow-up field visit that he completed high school and is in fact pursuing further studies at the Cape Technikon. A further lesson that one must never give up on young people – the possibility of a turn-around should be kept alive.

But in Phalo's case, it is too late. His violent death did not come as a surprise. He was no longer steering by the stars as he had lost sight of them as he went deeper and deeper into a drug culture in which violence became the only language of power. He gave up on his parents who could not provide for his basic needs in the form of food and clothing. He also felt strongly that they neither trusted nor respected him. In fact, he gave up on all adults. The peer group he fell back on consisted of equally desperate young men who sought solace in drugs because they could not live with themselves in a society they saw as hostile and uncaring. The price of peer support is often high. Demands for conformity, loyalty and demonstrations of love are insatiable under such circumstances. This is particularly pronounced in members of such groups who have psychological profiles reflecting poor self-image, mistrust and insecurity. It is not surprising that many like Phalo pay the ultimate price.

Young women seem to fare better than men in circumstances such as New Crossroads. Even though most families in the project exhibited instability of one form or another, most of the young women maintained a level of stability and achieved reasonable success. Even Lolo, who was abandoned by her mother and had to rely on her sister to protect her from their alcoholic father, seemed set for a reasonable adulthood. The presence of strong women in the community as well as the continuity of support she received from her sister and the tenant, Sisi Makoti, gave her positive role models. Her mediocre performance at school was likely to leave her unskilled, but women tend to accept lowly jobs more easily than men and thus to have access to a source of income, however small. Most women are able to survive and continue to support their families, probably because they lower their expectations and make the best of whatever comes their way. Of course this attitude is itself risky. A tolerance of abusive relationships at the personal and employment levels provides a poor role model for their daughters.

Many men, especially black men who have had to endure the humiliation of being treated as 'boys' by their white male counterparts, would rather starve than accept menial jobs. This response to adversity leads to further adversity as more and more men become unemployed and reliant on ever-diminishing returns of cash incomes from their womenfolk. The result is that women have to become ever stronger to keep their families alive and reasonably intact. Of course another consequence is that men become further disempowered by having to depend on the very women that a patriarchal culture designates as inferior to them. The dissonance between the cultural expectations of gender power relations on the one hand, and the reality of powerlessness on the other, sets off a vicious cycle of low self-esteem, resentment, anger and abuse of the very source of your support – the woman: mother, sister, wife, lover.

The current high level of gruesome violence against women is in part a reflection of this crisis in men. How else to explain sexual attacks on women, including baby girls? Especially when these are not necessarily by strangers, but more frequently by close friends and relatives? How to explain sexual violence by men against their own offspring? What else can explain the depravity of the gang rapes reported with such frightening regularity?

In the Limpopo Province where belief in witchcraft is rife, many women, particularly widowed women, are regularly brutally murdered by their own sons and close relatives who blame them for their own misfortunes. A woman who succeeds without the aid of a man is regarded with suspicion. How can a woman thrive where men have failed?

The sense of powerlessness, which is pervasive in some of the poor areas in this province, also encourages people to seek explanations for their misfortunes in the supernatural world. The widespread illiteracy and low levels of education add fuel to this fire of ignorance and fear. The problem has reached such alarming proportions that a protective village has been established by authorities west of Polokwane, to accommodate those fingered as witches.

There seems also to be an unwillingness on the part of the Limpopo government to clamp down on those involved in order to send a signal that such acts are criminal and intolerable. There is ambivalence toward dealing firmly with issues related to 'customs' – almost an unspoken fear that such firmness may be interpreted as an assault on 'African culture'. But there is nothing uniquely African about witch-hunts. Nor is it peculiar to African culture that women are singled out as witches to be burned at the stake or 'necklaced' as happens in many cases in South Africa. In times of upheavals and uncertainty, scapegoats are used to absorb the anger and fear of vulnerable communities. Europe had its turn during the Middle Ages. South Africa's transition to democracy is of such major proportions that it is bound to display these unstable tendencies that often lead to barbarism. But it is when good people remain silent that barbarism takes over. The law must be seen to be enforced at all times to curb this tendency.

It is the strength of black, especially African, women in situations such as these ravaged areas like New Crossroads that has kept a semblance of normality in families under siege from the legacy of racism, sexism and poverty. A lot more appreciation of this fact is needed to ensure that the implementation of social policies and the provision of services builds on, and supports, the strengths in women. Development that undermines women is bound to fail for this and many other reasons. There is fortunately growing recognition among people in development agencies that eliminating gender inequity is essential to sustainable development. Women are better managers of scarce resources, so enhancing their participation in socioeconomic and political decision-making is essential to the promotion of greater efficiency and effectiveness of public resources.

Indeed definitions of masculinity and femininity based on traditional norms are unhelpful to families on the edge of survival in the new South Africa. For one thing they limit the possibilities of young people modelling themselves on successful adults. A bolder step needs to be taken to free men and women from the shackles of traditionalism that have become dysfunctional in a modern society. It goes without saying that women would also need to be engaged in such a redefinition process.

VI

As a conclusion I would like to enumerate key elements essential for success in reinvigorating the three vital institutions – family, school, and community – essential to the healthy development of youth in our society. South Africa cannot afford to continue to let young people steer by the stars. They need to be provided with reliable compasses to enable them to develop self-confidence and face the future with hope.

We need to acknowledge the full extent of the legacy of apartheid and its socioeconomic consequences. The TRC only dealt with gross violation of human rights, but the violation of socioeconomic rights has left many communities disabled. Acknowledgement of this fact will contribute significantly to a relief from guilt of those victims of inequity who are made to feel that it is their fault that they are poor. Such acknowledgement need not be dramatised in the same manner as the TRC hearings, but concrete action to eradicate poverty will speak much louder than ritual.

The full extent of the impact of apartheid on society needs to be accepted. Families are in crisis. Schools are in crisis. Communities are in crisis. The triumphalism of the immediate post-apartheid period has led to a delay in appropriate interventions. There seems to be a discomfort in acknowledging the depth of the social crisis as if that would reflect badly on post-apartheid South Africa. But it is the failure to acknowledge the crisis that is reflecting badly on the society. How can others have confidence in the ability of society to tackle its problems if it denies their existence? The people cannot govern unless enabled to do so actively.

Traditional practices and customs that are dysfunctional to modernity and the democratic approaches embodied in our Constitution with its non-racial gender equity ideals need to be identified and challenged. Harmonisation of traditional practices with modernity is part of the normal human evolutionary process. African culture should not be seen as an exception in this instance as this can only impoverish it and lead to its eventual demise.

This vicious cycle of racism and fear of being stereotyped leads to failure for many black people who have been put in positions beyond their level of competence in post-apartheid South Africa. The cruel irony of the situation is that such failure is often used as evidence of black inferiority. The legacy of racism and the vicious cycle of stereotyping and the inferiority complex of some black people can only be broken by courageous leadership at all levels of society. The problem needs to be given a name and confronted.

Black people need to fight the enemy within that leads to self-doubt. They need to accept that they have not been accorded the opportunities to get the high-quality education and exposure to experiences that facilitate the honing of the critical skills needed at many levels in a modern society. They need to accept that lack of education and experience is not equivalent to an inferior intellect. Lack of knowledge is very different from stupidity. Lack of knowledge can be addressed by making opportunities available to all to develop their talents and close whatever skills' gaps that exist. But denial of the existence of skills' gaps makes personal development impossible.

White people also need to recognise how tainted they are by racism. There are still too many white people who believe that the leadership and privileged positions they are in are a reflection of their superior abilities compared to those below them with less education than they had. There is not enough consciousness of the benefits they have derived from one of the most successful affirmative action programmes in history. The world-class education white people had access to during the apartheid years was bought at the expense of a good education for their fellow citizens who happened to be black. The cost of redressing this imbalance has to be borne by society as a whole. An important starting point for white people is the acknowledgement of the legacy of racial discrimination, a commitment to work to banish racial stereotyping and to work with others to broaden the skills' base so urgently needed for successful transition to a prosperous democracy.

In the New Crossroads case the tragedy of this vicious cycle played itself out at various stages. The reluctance by the community to accept Alister Butler as director of the Youth Centre because he was a white man was part of the denial of the lack of skills within the community itself. His subsequent resignation resulted from being hounded out as an arrogant white man who also was suspected of teaching young people to be tolerant of homosexuality. He was neither arrogant nor a bad influence on young people. On the contrary, his dynamic leadership put the Youth Centre at the forefront of innovative ventures. But those fearing domination by white people were determined to get him out so that they could prove that they could run the facility on their own.

This attitude reflects a lack of appreciation of what it takes to establish and successfully run such a complex facility in an area of such great need. The reality was that the deputy director would have benefited from a longer period of working in a team with Butler to strengthen her management skills which were subsequently found wanting. It was this lack of management skills that finally led to the collapse of the Centre's programmes. The new director could not be faulted on creativity and initiative, but she just did not have an understanding of the importance of good management and team building to the long-term sustainability of any institution. Such management skills were even more needed given the lack of skills amongst the other members of staff she was meant to manage.

There seems to be little appreciation in this community and across many sectors of society that after hundreds of years of selective investment in white males it is inevitable that expertise and skills would be concentrated in that sector of the population. Recognition of this fact should not be confused with the myth of white male superiority. The strategic question confronting South Africa across all levels is how to gain maximum returns from this asset accumulated over the years of enforced discriminatory investment in white males for the benefit of all. One cannot wish away the reality of the skewed distribution of skills. What is required is to develop strategies that use these skills as a foundation to build a broader skills' base drawing on the widest pool of talent available.

Such a strategic approach requires courage to postpone the instant gratification of those previously excluded, whilst at the same time motivating those previously advantaged to see investing in broadening the skills' base as in their own long-term interests. Successful strategic management of this skills crisis requires visionary leadership at all levels of society. Black people have a legitimate expectation to see visible signs of transformation, including black people in leadership positions. However, sometimes self-gratification makes individuals claim competence beyond their ability in order to secure employment. Dealing with these issues is not easy.

White people, especially males, also face the challenge of confronting the insecurity and fears about their future in an environment in which they are seen to have an unfair advantage. Some have responded creatively and responsibly by acknowledging their position of advantage, without allowing themselves to be consumed by guilt. Such individuals – fortunately – represent a significant majority. They are actively engaged in activities that enable and support black men and women to develop their talents to the full. But there is also a significant minority trapped in fear and prejudice fuelling the vicious cycle of inferiority and superiority complexes which continue to undermine human development.

There is a silent white group that refrains from engagement in the reconstruction and development of their country for a number of reasons. Some could not be bothered – they have their privileges and believe that they owe nobody anything. Others are cynical about any prospect of successful transition to a non-racial democracy. They do not recognise how easy it is to turn such cynicism into a self-fulfilling prophecy. For as long as those with the skills hold back from engagement, for that long will society struggle to meet the challenges it faces, thus increasing the risk of failure. Still others are afraid to engage because they do not want to put a foot wrong and risk being labelled racist. Although one understands some of these fears, it is unreasonable for white South Africans to expect to live in a democratic non-racial society if they do not contribute actively to promoting the values that should guide such a prosperous democratic society. Their historical privilege places a responsibility on them to help resolve the legacy of apartheid.

South Africa's very future depends on the success with which everyone tackles these challenges.

Where are they now?

BULELWA is now 24 years old and divorced. She and her child once again live in New Crossroads, with her mother and sisters and their two children. She works for a major insurance company as a client consultant.

BULELANI is now 26 years old. He is single and has no children and lives with his mother and nephew in New Crossroads. In 1999 he graduated from a local technikon after qualifying as a civil engineer and he works for an engineering company in Cape Town. He is not satisfied with his job and aims to gain further qualifications and to study abroad.

LOLO is now 20 years old and lives in New Crossroads with her mother, two brothers and three sisters. After matriculating two years ago, she intended continuing with her studies but lack of finances prevented this. Recently she suffered from a debilitating infection of the kidneys which cost her a job as a salesperson at a furniture store. She has since recovered and is looking for employment. She thinks back fondly to the weekend trails.

DUMO is now 24 years old. After passing Grade 11 he found himself in financial difficulties and was forced to find work. He was employed by a delivery company for a number of years but lost this job when he went to circumcision school. He now helps his mother run a small spaza shop in New Crossroads and is saving to continue his education.

LUNGA is now 25 years old. After failing matric he dropped out of school and went to work as a driver for a chauffeuring company. Two years ago he was arrested for riding in a stolen car and is currently in Pollsmoor prison awaiting trial.

XOLA is now 22 years old and living with his mother, sister and two nieces in New Crossroads. He left school during his Grade 11 year because of gang related problems, but ploughed his energies into teaching and aftercare for young children. He also teaches dancing and coaches older children in various sporting activities. Xola and five others have formed an outreach group and are sponsored by the Amy Biehl Foundation. They offer programmes at the premises of the two local government primary schools.

MTHETHELELI is now 22 years old and lives with his mother, two sisters and a brother in New Crossroads. He matriculated in 2000 with good results and received a bursary from the Institute of Race Relations. This has enabled him to study environmental health at a local technikon. He feels that the project contributed directly to his educational success.

NANA is now 23 years old and currently rewriting two of her matric subjects by correspondence. Like her sister and brother, she is unemployed and the three of them live with their father in New Crossroads. Their mother left him five years ago. He is still drinking as badly as he was during the project, but continues to support the family on his income as a taxi driver.

TULEKA is now 25 years old. After matriculating in 1994, she studied marketing management and found temporary jobs at various companies. When she couldn't find a permanent position she moved to East London but found the employment market as difficult there. She has since returned to Cape Town and is looking for a job. She lives with her father and two younger sisters in New Crossroads. Tuleka feels frustrated that her dreams have not worked out. She had hoped to earn enough money to educate her sisters.

THABO is now 21 years old. He and his girlfriend and their two children live with his mother and his younger brother in New Crossroads. He was forced to drop out of school for financial reasons. He has found a job as a cashier at a garage and is doing well. He plans to continue his studies as soon as he can find a job that does not involve shift work.

PULE is now 23 years old. Financial difficulties forced her to drop out of school after passing Grade 11, but since then she been empoyed as a cashier at a supermarket. This has allowed her to save some money. In addition it has helped support her grandmother and four cousins in their house in New Crossroads. Like Thabo she wants to find work that does not entail shifts in order to continue her studies.

BOBO is now 21 years old. She matriculated in 2000 but has been unable to find a job. She feels frustrated at not even having enough money to look for a job and is considering going back to school to improve her matric. She lives with her parents and two brothers in New Crossroads.

NONO is now 18 years old and expecting her first child. After passing Grade 11, she left school to do a course on home nursing and caring for abused children. She works as a volunteer in this field and would like to qualify as a nurse eventually. She lives with her mother and two brothers in New Crossroads. Her mother is the sole breadwinner.

TOMELA is now 23 years old. He lives with his mother, two brothers and his child in New Crossroads. His father left the household when Tomela was in Grade 7, forcing him to drop out of school to take care of his mother and younger brothers. He is a taxi driver.

TUMI is now 21 years old. Financial difficulties forced her mother to sell the house and the family moved to the Eastern Cape. Tumi dropped out of school in her Grade 10 year. Conditions in the Eastern Cape were as dire and the family returned to Cape Town. They are now living in the KTC squatter settlement. Tumi works at a restaurant as a dishwasher, part of her wage going to support her mother, two cousins and three sisters.

Bibliography

Amit-Talai, V and Wulff, H (eds.), *Youth Culture: A Cross-Cultural Perspective*, London: Routledge, 1995.

Anderson, B, *Imagined Communities: Reflections on the Origin and Spread of Nationalism,* London: Verso, 1983.

Behar, R, *The Vulnerable Observer: Anthropology That Breaks Your Heart*, Boston: Beacon Press, 1997.

Berk, L, *Child Development,* Boston: Allyn and Beacon, 1997.

Bell, C and Newby, H, *Community Studies: An Introduction to the Local Community,* London: George Allen and Unwin, 1971.

Bernstein, P L, *Against the Gods: The Remarkable Story of Risk*, New York: Wiley & Sons, 1996.

Bradshaw, D, 'Review of South African Mortality (1984)', in *Technical Report,* 1, South Africa: Medical Research Council, 1987.

Bundy, C, *At War with the Future? Black South African Youth in the 1990s,* Cape Town: Institute for Historical Research, University of the Western Cape, 1993.

Burman, S and Reynolds, P (eds.), *Growing Up in a Divided Society: The Contexts of Childhood in South Africa,* Johannesburg: Ravan Press, 1986.

Campbell, C, 'Social Change and Intergenerational Conflict in Township Families', in Mason, J et al. (eds.), *From Diversity to Healing,* Durban: SAIMF, 1992.

Cape Argus, 18 September 1997, 'Youth Reap Violent Harvest of Apartheid's Repression'.

Cape Times, 09 November 1998, 'Crowd Dispenses "Justice"'.

Cathsoc, *Crossroads,* Johannesburg: WITS Cathsoc Publication, 1988.

Childhood, 5,1, London: Sage Publications, 1998.

Clifford, J and Marcus, G (eds.), *Writing Culture: The Poetics and Politics of Ethnography,* Berkeley: University of California, 1986.

Clinton, H, *It Takes a Village and Other Lessons Children Teach Us,* New York: Simon & Schuster, 1996.

Cole, J, *Crossroads: The Politics of Reform and Repression 1976-1986,* Johannesburg: Ravan Press, 1987.

Cooksey, E, Menaghan, E and Jekielek, S, 'Life Course Effects of Work and Family Circumstances on Children', *Social Forces,* 76,2, 1997.

Cooper, P, Molteno, C, Murray, L and Swartz, L, 'Social Adversity, Maternal Mental State and Infant Emotional, Cognitive, and Physical Outcome: An Epidemiological Survey and an Intervention Study in Khayelitsha, South Africa', Draft Protocol Paper, 1995.

Crockett, L and Crouter, A (eds.), *Pathways through Adolescence: Individual Development in Relation to Social Contexts,* New Jersey: Lawrence Eribaum Associated Publishers, 1995.

Dale, P, *The Myth of Japanese Uniqueness*, New York: Routledge, 1986.

Dawes, A and Donald, D, *Childhood and Diversity: Psychological Perspectives from South African Research*, Cape Town: David Philip, 1994.

De Haas, M, 'Putting Their Money Where Their Mouths Are: Policy Makers, Professionals and the Political Realities of African Family Life in Natal', in Mason, J et al., *From Diversity to Healing,* Durban: SAIMF, 1992.

Dewar, D, Rosmarin, T, and Watson, V, 'Movement Patterns of the African Population in Cape Town', *UPRU Working Paper,* 44, Cape Town: UPRU, 1991.

Dornbusch, S M et al., 'The Relation of Parenting Style to Adolescent School Performance', *Child Development*, 58, 1987.

Doyle, P et al., *Towards Optimisation of the HIV Modelling Process in South Africa*, Natal University Press, 1998.

Drost, A, Gray, D and Howie, S, 'Mathematics and Science Performance in the Middle School Years in South Africa: A Summary Report on the Performance of South African Students', in the *Third International Mathematics and Science Study* (TIMSS), Pretoria: HSRC, 1997.

Education Foundation, *School Register of Needs*, Pretoria: HSRC, 1997.

Erickson, E, *Insight and Responsibility*, New York: W.W. Norton, 1964.

Erikson, E, *Identity: Youth and Crisis*, New York: W.W. Norton, 1968.

Everatt, D (ed.), *Creating a Future: Youth Policy in the New South Africa*, Johannesburg: Ravan Press, 1994.

Everatt, D and Orkin, M, *Growing up Tough: A National Survey of South African Youth,* Johannesburg: CASE, 1993.

Everatt, D and Sisulu, E (eds.), *Black Youth in Crisis: Facing the Future*, Johannesburg: Ravan Press, 1992.

Ewen, A (ed.), *Voice of Indigenous Peoples: Native People Address the United Nations,* Santa Fe: Clear Light Publishers, 1994.

Fine, G A, 'Friends, Impression Management, and Preadolescent Behaviour', in *The Development of Children's Friendships*, New York: Cambridge University Press, 1981.

Freeman, D, *Margaret Mead and Samoa*, Cambridge: Harvard University Press, 1983.

Garmezy, N, 'Resiliency and Vulnerability to Adverse Development Outcomes Associated with Poverty', *American Behavioural Scientist*, 34, 1991, pp. 416-430.

Gibbs, J T, *Young, Black and American: An Endangered Species*, Dover, MA: Auburn Press, 1988.

Giddens, A, *Modernity and Self-Identity: Self and Society in the Late Modern Age*, Great Britain: Polity Press, 1991.

Gillis, R, *A World of Their Own Making: A History of Myth and Ritual in Family Life*. Oxford: Oxford University Press, 1997.

Guyer, J, 'Household and Community in African studies', *African Studies Review*, 24, 1-2, 1981.

Hauser, S T and Bolwds, M K, 'Family Interiors of Adolescent Ego Development', *Child Development*, Vol. 55, 1987.

Hauser, S T, Powers, S I and Noam, G G, *Adolescents and Their Families: Paths of Ego Development*, New York: Book News, 1991.

Harris, K and Marmer, J, 'Poverty, Paternal Involvement and Adolescent Well-Being', *Journal of Family Issues*, Sage Publications, 1996.

Henderson, V L and Dweck, C S, 'Motivation and Achievement in Adolescence: Toward a Model of Motivational Processes', in Feldman, S S and Elliot, G R (eds.), *At the Threshold: The Development Adolescent*, Cambridge: Harvard University Press, 1990.

Herzfeld, Michael, *Anthropology Through the Looking Glass*, New York: Cambridge University Press, 1987.

Holliday, L, *Children of 'The Troubles'*, New York: Pocket Books, 1997.

Houghton, W, *The Victorian Frame of Mind*, New Haven: Yale University Press, 1957.

Howie, S and Hughes, C, 'Mathematics and Science Literacy of Final-Year School Students in South Africa: A Report on the Performance of South African Students', in the *Third International Mathematics and Science Study* (TIMSS), Pretoria: HSRC.

Huchzermeyer, M, 'Nyanga: Interviewing of Residents and Role-Players', Draft Paper, 1996.

Hurrelmann, K and Engel, V (eds.), *The Social World of Adolescents: International Perspectives*, New York: De Gruyter, 1989.

Hymes, D, *Ethnography, Linguistics, Narrative Inequality: Toward an Understanding of Voice*, Washington, DC: Taylor & Francis, 1996.

Independent Develoment Trust Annual Reports, 1990-1997.

James, W and Simons, M, *The Angry Divide: Social and Economic History of the Western Cape*, Cape Town: David Philip, 1989.

Jennings, R and Everatt, D, *Hewers of Wood and Drawers of Water? Analyzing the Needs of 'Out-of-school' Youth in South Africa*, Johannesburg: CASE, 1995.

Jones, R, *Black Adolescents*, California: Cobb and Henry Publishers, 1989.

Kabeer, N, *Reversed Realities: Gender Hierarchies in Development Thought*, London: Verso, 1994.

Laerke, A, 'By Means of Re-remembering: Notes on a Fieldwork with English Children', *Anthropology Today*, 14,1, 1998.

Lawuyi, O B, 'Anthropology in South Africa: The Need for Change and the Change of Need', *South African Journal of Ethnology*, 20,2, 1997.

Leading Edge, 2, Special Focus on Youth, 1994.

Liebow, E, *Tally's Corner*, Boston: Little, Brown and Company, 1967.

Lindholm, C, 'Logical and Moral Dilemmas of Postmodernism', *Journal of the Royal Anthropological Institute*, 3,4, 1997.

Magwaza, A, 'Psychosocial Crisis in South African Black Migrant Families: A Systemic Approach', in Mason,T et al. (eds.), *From Diversity to Healing*, Durban: SAIMF, 1992.

Manganaro, M, *Myth, Rhetoric, and the Voice of Authority*, New Haven: Yale University Press, 1992.

Marcus, G E and Fischer, M J, *Anthropology as Cultural Critique: An Experimental moment in the Human Sciences*, Chicago: University of Chicago Press, 1986.

Mason,T, Rubenstein, J, and Shuda, S (eds.), *From Diversity to Healing: Papers from the 5th Biennial International Conference of the South African Institute of Marital and Family Therapy*, Durban: SAIMF, 1992.

Mazrui, A A, *The Africans: A Triple Heritage*, Boston: Little, Brown and Company, 1986.

Meeus, W, 'Parental and Peer Support', in Hurrelmann, K and Engel, V (eds.), *The Social World of Adolescents: International Perspectives*, New York: De Gruyter, 1989.

Milkie, M, Simon, R and Powell, B, 'Through the Eyes of Children: Youth's Perceptions and Evaluation of Maternal and Paternal Roles', *Social Psychology Quarterly* 60,3, 1997.

Mill, J S, *Essays in Politics and Culture,* Himmelfarb, G (ed.), New York: Doubleday, 1963.

Millstein, S, Petersen, A and Nightingale, E, *Promoting the Health of Adolescents: New Directions for the Twenty-First Century,* New York: Oxford University Press, 1993.

Mitscherlich, A, *Society Without the Father*, New York: Harper Press, 1993.

Mitterauer, M, *A History of Youth,* Oxford: Blackwell, 1993.

Moody, R, *The Indigenous Voice: Visions and Realities*, London: Zed Books, 1988.

Moore, H, 'Interior Landscapes and External Worlds: The Return of Grand Theory in Anthropology', *The Australian Journal of Anthropology*, 8,2, 1997.

Moore, H, *A passion for Difference: Essays in Anthropology and Gender*, Cambridge: Polity Press, 1994.

Moore, J, *Visions of Culture: An Introduction to Anthropological Theories and Theorists*, London: Altamira Press, 1997.

Moore, M, Sixsmith, J and Knowles, K, *Children's Reflections on Family Life*, London: Falmer Press, 1996.

Moser, C, *Confronting Crisis: A Comparative Study of Household Responses to Poverty and Vulnerability in Four Poor Urban Communities*, Washington: World Bank, 1996.

Moser, C, and Holland, J, *Urban Poverty and Violence in Jamaica*, Washington: World Bank, 1997.

Murray, C, *Families Divided*, Ravan Press: Johannesburg, 1981.

Nene, D S, 'Decision Making and Power Relations within Black Families: A Search for Theory and Research Programme', Durban: ASSA conference, 1988.

Nightingale, C H, *On The Edge*, New York: Basic Books, 1993.

Nisbert, R, *The Sociological Tradition*, New York: Basic Books, 1967.

Nuttall, J, *The First Five-Years: The Story of the Independent Development Trust*, Cape Town: IDT, 1985.

Nzimande, B, Opening Speech at Joint Education Programme Conference on 'Marginalised' Youth, 1991.

ODA Working Paper, 12, 'Townships in Cape Town: A Pilot Study of Nyanga, New Crossroads and KTC', Newcastle: CARDO, 1996.

ODA Working Paper, 13, 'Nyanga Township: A Case Study of its People, Living Environment and Development Potentials', Newcastle: CARDO, 1997.

Parsons, T, Shils, E, Naegele, K and Pitts, J (eds.), *Theories of Society: Foundations for Modern Sociological Theory*, New York: Free Press, 1965.

Ramphele, M, *Adolescence and Violence in South Africa*, Working Paper 3, Series on International Mental and Behavioural Health, Programme in Medical Anthropology, Harvard University, 1993.

Ramphele, M, *A Bed Called Home: Life in the Migrant Labour Hostels of Cape Town*, Cape Town: David Philip,1993.

Ramphele, M, 'South African Youth: Millstone or Opportunity?' *Leading Edge*, 2, Special Focus on Youth, Cape Town: IDT, 1994.

173

Ramphele, M A and Thorton, R, 'The quest for community', in Boonzaier, E and Sharp, J, *South African Keywords: The Uses and Abuses of Political Concepts,* Cape Town: David Philip, 1988.

Ramphele, M A, Heap, M and Trollip, D K, 'A Survey of the Physical Health Status of Pupils Aged 10-14 Years in Standards 3-5 at three Schools in New Crossroads, Near Cape Town in the Western Cape', *South African Medical Journal,* 85,10, 1995.

Ravi Prasat, D M, *Dalit Youth: A Sociological Study,* New Delhi: A P H Publishing Corporation, 1997.

Reynolds, P, *Childhood in Crossroads: Cognition and Society in South Africa,* Cape Town: David Philip, 1989.

Reynolds, P, 'Youth and the Politics of Culture in South Africa', in Stephens, S (ed.), *Children and the Politics of Culture,* New Jersey: Princeton University Press, 1995.

Ritcher, L, 'Economic Stress and its Influence on the Family and Caretaking Patterns', in Dawes, A and Donald, D, *Childhood and Adversity: Psychological Perspectives from South African Research,* Cape Town: David Philip, 1994.

Robertson, G and De Kiewit, S, 'Wilderness Therapy with Militarised Youth in Traumatised Communities', *Journal of Social Development in Africa,* 13,1, 1998.

Roche, J and Tucker, S (eds.), *Youth in Society: Contemporary Theory, Policy and Practice,* London: Sage Publications, 1997.

SALDRU, *South Africa Rich and Poor: Baseline Household Statistics,* Project for Statistics on Living Standards and Development, Cape Town: SALDRU, 1994.

Salmon, M H, 'Ethical considerations in Anthropology and Archaeology, or Relativism and Justice for All', *Journal of Anthropological Research,* 53,1, 1997.

Schlegel, A and Barry, H, *Family and Adolescents: An Anthropological Inquiry,* New York: Free Press, 1991.

Scott, R and Scott, W A, *Adjustment of Adolescents – Cross-cultural Similarities and Differences,* London: Routledge, 1998.

Seekings, J, *Heroes or Villans? Youth Politics in the 1980s,* Johannesburg: Ravan Press, 1993.

Seekings, J, 'South Africa's Youth: A "Lost Generation"?', pamphlet, 1994.

Seleoane, M, *Nyanga East Men's Hostels: The Condition of Migrant Workers,* Cape Town: SALDRU, 1985.

Sharp, J and Spiegel, A, *Vulnerability to Impoverishment in South African Rural Areas: The Erosion of Kinship and Neighbourhood as Social Resources,* Cape Town: SALDRU, 1984.

Silverstein, K, *Children of the Dark Ghetto,* New York: Praeger Press, 1975.

Skinner, D, *Apartheid's Violent Legacy: A Report on Trauma in the Western Cape*, Cape Town: The Trauma Centre, 1998.

Steele, C, 'Race and the Schooling of Black Americans', *The Atlantic Monthly*, April 1992.

Straker, G, *Faces in the Revolution: The Psychological Effects of Violence on Township Youth in South Africa*, Cape Town: David Philip, 1992.

Sulloway, F, *Born to Rebel: Birth Order, Family Dynamics and Creative Lives*, New York: Pantheon Books, 1996.

Suskind, R, *A Hope in the Unseen: An American Odyssey from the Inner City to the Ivy League*, New York: Broadway Books, 1998.

Takanishi, R and Hamburg, D (eds.), *Preparing Adolescents for the 21st Century*, Cambridge: Cambridge University Press, 1997.

Taylor, R L, 'Black Youth, Role Models and the Social Construction of Identity', in Jones, R, *Black Adolescents*, California: Cobb and Henry Publishers, 1989.

Track Two, 'Bringing Youth in from the Margins', 7,3, Cape Town: Centre for Conflict Resolution/ Media Peace Centre, 1998.

Van de Vliet, V, 'Staying Single, A Strategy Against Poverty', Carnegie Conference Paper, Cape Town: SALDRU, 1984.

Van Zyl Slabbert, F, et al. (eds.), *Youth in the New South Africa*, Pretoria: HSRC, 1994.

Walaza, N, *Programme Report on Violence and Intervention Programme for Youth in New Crossroads*, Cape Town: Urban Violence Project, 1998.

Weekend Argus 20/09/1997, 'Gangland Kids Sent Far Afield to Escape Violence'.

Weekly Mail & Guardian, 4-10/04/1997, 'Police Ignore the Rape of Four-Year-Old Girl'.

Werner, E E and Smith, R S, *Vulnerable but Invincible: A Longitudinal Study of Resilient Children and Youth*, New York: McGraw Hill, 1983.

West, C, *Restoring Hope*. Boston: Beacon Press, 1997.

Western, J, *Outcast in Cape Town*, Berkeley: University of California Press, 1996.

Whitaker, M, 'Ethnography as Learning: A Wittgensteinian Approach to Writing Ethnographic Accounts', *Anthropological Quarterly*, 69,1, 1996.

Whitbeck, L, Simons, R, Conger, R, Wickrama, K, Ackley, K and Elder, G, 'The Effects of Parents' Working Conditions and Family Economic Hardship on Parenting Behaviours and Children's Self-Efficacy', *Social Psychological Quarterly*, 60,4, 1997.

Wilson, E, *Consilience: The Unity of Knowledge*, Little, Brown and Company, 1999.

Wilson, F, *Labour in the South African Gold Mines 1911-1969*, Cambridge: Cambridge University Press, 1972.

Wilson, F and Ramphele, M, *Uprooting Poverty: The South African Challenge*, Cape Town: David Philip, 1989.

Wilson, J W, *The Truly Disadvantaged: The Inner City, the Underclass, and Public Policy,* Chicago: University of Chicago Press, 1987.

Wilson, M, *For Men and Elders,* London: International African Institute, 1977.

Wood, K, Maforah, F and Jeukes, R, *Sex, Violence and Construction of Love among Xhosa Adolescents: Putting Violence on the Sexuality Education Agenda,* Cape Town: CERSA, 1996.

Wyn, J and White, R, *Rethinking Youth*, London: Sage Publications, 1997.

Yach, D, *Paediatrics Tables*, Centre for Epidemiological Research in Southern Africa, Medical Research Council, mimeo, 1988.

Zechenter, E, 'In the Name of Culture: Cultural Relativism and the Abuse of the Individual', *Journal of Anthropological Research,* 53, 1997.